NOTHING SERIOUS, I HOPE

by

Maynard Good Stoddard

OWEN COUNTY PUBLIC LIBRARY
10 SOUTH MONTGOMERY STREET
SPENCER, IN 47460
812-829-3392

© 2001 by Maynard Good Stoddard. All rights reserved.

No part of this book may be reproduced, stored in a retrieval system, or transmitted by any means, electronic, mechanical, photocopying, recording, or otherwise, without written permission from the author.

ISBN: 0-7596-5819-6

This book is printed on acid free paper.

1stBooks – rev. 11/03/01

ACKNOWLEDGMENT

I remain well aware that I have already centered recognition for my labors on the woman who has dwelt under the same roof with me for the past 65 years (which seem more like 66). But after reviewing the contents of <u>Nothing Serious, I Hope</u>, upon who else could I lay the blame?

I refer--if you'd care to browse--to chapters such as:

The Trouble with Zippers
Knit 1, Purl 2, Hubby o
Women and Gasoline don't Mix
Off to work She Goes
Try Not to Bleed
Do You Take This Man?--and How!
Wake Up, It's Time to Go to Bed
On Satin Sheets

You get the idea. And it'll be a cold dinner for me upon publication day. If there's a dinner at all.

NOTHING SERIOUS, I HOPE dedication:
To Our Ambitious Grandsons

Robert Gaven Kristopher

Chapter 1

TENSION, ANYONE?

If this doctor is not just talking through his stethoscope, I stand a good chance of living indefinitely. Perhaps longer. He says that tension, rather than shortening life, actually strengthens the old ticker and allows it to take a licking and keep on ticking. And if he's right, most of the credit for my longevity must go, in all fairness, to the proverbial woman behind every successful man.

Had it not been for this proverbial woman, I could very well have gone to an early grave direct from our snug little apartment in the city. Here, tensions rose to fever pitch but twice a year: in the spring at birdbath-painting time, and again in midsummer with the screwdriving of grass from between the bricks on the patio. But thanks to little proverbial's having evidently been given a transfusion of Gypsy blood before we met, we now reside on a 13-acre hilltop view with attached house at Freedom, Indiana. And according to the doc's theory, our first winter here alone toned up my ticker until the only way it'll stop ticking is for someone to take it out and beat it with a club. If someone can catch it, that is.

To my good health, our move happened to coincide with the heaviest snowfall in the county's history. Snow, in fact, reached its highest depth (don't dwell on "highest depth" too long or you'll go nuts) the day we drove home—or toward home—from Spencer with a week's supply of groceries. And, boy oh boy, the car couldn't make it up our winding drive. The reason was, our car got stuck at the foot of the hill on Big Four Road leading up *to* our winding drive. Thus I was provided the wholesome chore of slogging half a mile through snow up to my frozen wazoo supporting two bags of groceries with each arm. And whenever monotony would begin to slow the old pump, I'd rev it up by depositing the bags in the snow and floundering back to unclog the woman who had promoted the move from our snug little city apartment.

When the bottoms of the sacks began giving out, I was concerned that they might lighten to the point of unstimulation. But not to worry. I spent a most salubrious afternoon with a bushel basket, gathering what I could find of the stuff. The last of the cans had to wait for the snow to melt in early March, giving us the added thrill of surprise when they were opened, the wrappers having long since disappeared.

That very night, providentially, the water pipes froze.

Maynard Good Stoddard

This provided an excuse for wallowing a half-mile down the hill in the opposite direction to a year-round flowing well along old Route 67, filling four plastic milk jugs and wallowing home. After my fifth such invigorator, a feeling of guilt forced me to invite my dear wife to extend her own life span a few years by taking a turn. Selfless to a fault, she declined.

The number of decades beyond my current six that I will owe to the failure of the oil delivery truck to make it up the hill, I can't begin to estimate. But in counting my blessings, among the top ten surely must go the day the tank ran dry and I fell heir to the heart-strengthening situation of having to dig out the car, buck the drifts into Spencer, fill two five-gallon cans with fuel oil, buck back to our snow carport and drag the cans up the hill to the tank. Daily.

I remember mumbling to my dear wife as she was prying my hands loose from the handles after one such bracer, "Surely a man could ask for nothing more."

But as they say, them that has, gets.

Salutary as present conditions now stood, it remains for the night the mercury plummeted to 24 below, the oil line jelled and the furnace shut off completely, to make me fully appreciate just what a health spa we really had. Even then, particularly around midnight, when we would leave the haven of the open oven door in the kitchen and head, tensely, for the icy sheets in the bedroom, I'm embarrassed to confess that I didn't acknowledge to my dear wife even once that it was only due to her keen foresight in getting out of that snug little Indianapolis apartment that my heart of 60 summers was having such a field day.

How I dreaded the threat of spring. In my despondency over losing the cold and the snow, all I could visualize ahead was life-shortening warm weather, a negotiable driveway, the serenity of sitting on the front porch looking out over an acre of freshly mown lawn or relaxing on the back patio watching our groceries growing on the half-acre garden. But, like most fears, the apprehension turned out to be worse than the reality.

In fact, just trying to stay on a riding mower traversing a 40-degree slope (the Sears man said it was their first incidence of having a riding mower seat worn out under warranty) soon gave me to know that I had nothing to fear but fear itself. If there were any doubts, they went with the initial launching of the Rototiller, with which I had hoped to make our garden soil somewhat more receptive to seeds. The topsoil had left our garden for the valley, you see, shortly after the world was created. What we have left is clay. Not your ordinary common everyday pottery clay, but clay, the type of clay from which bowling balls must be made.

Taking nothing away from the tiller, I feel that I deserve some of the credit for the minimum of five years this lovely contraption added to my regulation four score and seven (or is that the Gettysburg Address?). Had I understood that an adjustment must be made before the blades stood any chance at all of penetrating our so-called soil, my dear wife might well be fluffing up my deathbed pillow right now. As it was, we—the tiller and I—were doing at least 35 miles an hour when we caromed off the birdbath at the end of the garden and leveled my dear wife's newly planted French lilac. I stayed with it, toning up the old ticker all the way across the backyard and over the two dwarf pear trees. But when my shin caught the saw horse behind the shed and my knee took down the woodpile, I decided to let the tiller tackle the grape arbor alone. Too much of a good thing might be worse than none at all.

Right about here that young 40-year-old in the back row will be thinking, Sure, that's all well and good for you, but *my* wife doesn't have Gypsy blood in her crankcase, we don't live on a hill, we don't have bowling-ball clay for topsoil and, woe is me, *I* am doomed to an early grave.

Not necessarily. Statistics prove that just the normal tension of a married man's environment gives him many years' advantage over the poor unharassed bachelor. True, such things as Rototillers can provide the big booster shot, but the accumulative effect of daily married life will also keep a man's heart right up there in his mouth, its most healthful location in the body.

Take the seemingly minor incident of my own dear wife joining me for a siesta one day this summer direct from painting the shed.

Planning to add a second coat when she woke up, she hadn't bothered to remove samples of the first coat from her hands before tucking in. So when I woke up, without my glasses, and saw this "thing" with its horrible red and white tentacles wriggling on the pillow, my heart was bolstered to the point of grabbing up the book I'd been reading and getting in three lusty whacks before she rose up screaming.

"It's all right!" I screamed back. "I think I've killed it!"
"So do I," she moaned, sticking her "tentacles" under her arm and rocking back and forth.

Maynard Good Stoddard

I was quick to point out that she was lucky I'd been reading a paperback and not the *Complete Works of Charles Dickens,* but even then the ensuing tension held me nicely into the next day.

While I am willing to admit that were it not for my dear wife she would likely be a widow by now (you may need a little extra time to think about that), the lady called Luck is equally dependable when it comes to keeping a man's throbber throbbing. I refer to the chance blessings of such things as wasps infesting your attic, bats inhabiting your chimney or maybe a woodchuck chucking on the timbers beneath your house.

The chance blessing I am most familiar with is the woodchuck beneath the house.

We have a full ten acres of woods for this animal to chuck in. But, as luck would have it, he chose instead to do it on the supporting lumber directly beneath our bedroom. And if racket denotes progress, he should be coming up through the floor any day now. If it should occur during our siesta (I may refer the question to Ann Landers), would it be proper for the man to precede his wife through the bedroom ceiling?

It was only after several days of gnawing that I learned to which species of vermin I would owe these additional years of life. But we could set our clocks by it. Promptly at 1 p.m. the chomping would begin. At around 2:30, depending on how many times I would leave my typewriter or my wife her crochet hook to go in and tap, gingerly, on the floor, it would end. Then one day I happened to be standing at the window gathering nouns when this animal came squeezing out from under the shed, surveyed the scene from tippytoe on his hind legs and headed for the house. The time: 12:59. The mystery was a mystery no longer.

Son Michael, living away from home and owning more guns than he can shoot at one time, insisted on lending me one of his pistols, or revolvers, or whatever—I don't know the first thing about guns, much less the second. This particular weapon held several bullets in a gadget which he showed me how to insert, a cocking formula which he demonstrated, twice, and a "safety" gizmo which he explained at some length. I put the box containing the gun on the dresser. Ever so carefully. And there I was sure it would stay.

But the very next day I was to catch Mr. Woodchuck flatfooted on his regular commune from shed to house. My heart leaped within me.

Streaking into the bedroom, I unboxed the pistol, revolver, or whatever, dashed into the kitchen to have wife refresh my memory on the cocking procedure, slipped out the front door, sneaked up to the corner of the house and came charging back into the kitchen to get straightened out on releasing the safety.

By the time I returned to the corner of my house, my prey, having smelled, or heard, a rat, was hightailing it for the safety of the shed. Drawing a careful bead and shutting my eyes, I scored a clean hit on the fuel oil tank. Low down. Filled only the previous week, at 91.2 cents per gallon.

Trying to keep a finger stuck in the hole while snapping off another round, I believe it's called, I missed everything but the right front tire on our '72 skylark, parked for the first time that day beside the shed to protect it from the afternoon sun. The explosion of the tire prompted the woodchuck to reverse its field and head back for the house. This in turn prompted me to remove most of my finger from the hole in the tank and make for the side door. To my recollection, it's the first time I had ever gone through a screen door without opening it.

"What was all the rush?" asked my dear wife, trying to work the remains of the door back over my ears.

"I needed a clothespin for the fuel oil tank," I explained, without bothering to explain.

Even for a married man there will be times, of course, when all is well and he'll find himself just sitting around in the quiet listening to his heart pitter-patting his life away. I ran into such a stretch for a couple of hours right after the woodchuck episode.

A clothespin plugged the hole in the fuel oil tank. The spare tire had been mounted on the right front. The gun lay safely nestled in its box on the dresser. The woodchuck had departed for less disturbing climes. We have decided to go the easy route and convert the garden into a clay tennis court. And most of the screen segments had been removed from my forehead. Thankfully, however, my wise and wonderful wife had anticipated this possible threat to my well-being and bought two Nubian goats, trying to conceal her sentimentality behind the flimsy explanation that they would keep the poison ivy off the back fence.

The fact that they still have half the flower bed, a little of the grape arbor and about an hour's work left on the bark of the two new dwarf pear trees to go before reaching their intended target is beside the point. The point is, wonderful

Maynard Good Stoddard

little wife has just rushed in to announce that the little rascals have pulled my pants off the line where they were drying after I'd tried watering the lawn with a hose the chipmunks had chewed into, and they are headed for the woods, dragging my pants behind them. My car keys are—or were—in one of the pockets.

I can feel the old pump picking up that life-prolonging tempo already.

Chapter 2

MACRAME IS A HEADACHE

My best feature has always been a well-shaped head. I've often wished that heads were a category at the state fair so I could enter mine. But no longer. Thanks to my wife's enthusiastic endorsement of the current craze of hanging flower pots from the ceiling, my head now corresponds pretty much to the contours of the Hubbard squash.

Not that I am placing the blame on macrame per se. According to my dictionary, macrame is, or *was*, nothing more menacing than "a fringe, lace or trimming of knotted thread or cord...a kind of decoration on hand towels." Nowhere do I find a justification for its use as a sling for crocks full of dirt hoisted to the proper level for beating a man's brains out. Or, at best, a jungle to beat his way through on a safari to the bathroom.

My wife had always been content crocheting doilies and knitting sweaters.

"Isn't that stitch a bit loose for a sweater?" I remember asking, the night she launched the original project.

"It's not a sweater," she answered mischievously.
"A hammock for the dog?" I joked, little realizing its lethal potential.
"You'll see," she said, with what I took to be another mischievous twinkle but more than likely was a gleam of anticipation at the delightful moment when I would crack my cranium on her camouflaged birdcage for the very first time. Nor was I about to disappoint her.

It's not that I am overly tall. I *might* have been a little overly tall before all the punishment my head has taken, but even with my latest lumps I'm still a shade under six feet. The trouble is, my wife stands five-five, in heels. This means that suspended crockery that she can clear comfortably catches me just above the eyebrows. Depending upon the consistency of the container—they vary, I have found, from papier-mache to cast iron—I can wobble away with anything from a protrusion to a contusion to a concussion.

Anyway, the day of my introduction to macrame, I came bounding joyously into the house as usual, proceeded to drop my brief case just inside the doorway, grabbed my head and staggered to the sofa. My wife, feigning innocence, looked in to ask what kind of day I'd had. I told her, upon regaining my ability to talk, that in retrospect the day had gone well. Following an emotional struggle, I added that she might consider elevating her lovely bucket of trailing arbutus just a smidgeon.

"I don't mean way up where I won't still have to fight my way through the foliage or anything that drastic," I quickly interjected. "But maybe high enough to keep the part in my hair from originating beneath my scalp."

She replied, rather coolly, I thought, that she had spent no little time positioning her handicraft for maximum impact. Especially on anyone over five-five, I should have retorted. But I'm one of those people to whom retorts usually come a day late.

As with other vices, once hooked, she couldn't stop flat out cold. Especially not when the results were proving so effective. Ergo, on my third day of bouncing off the original booby trap in the hallway, I had no more than recovered my bearings when I was brought to my knees by a second arrangement strategically hung in my path to the refrigerator.

After that there was no stopping her.

There are those, of course, who will say, "Anyone with half a brain wouldn't require three days to begin avoiding those cranium crushers." The key phrase here is "half a brain." A brain battered for three days is lucky to retain a record of which house its master belongs in, much less the Hanging Gardens of Mayhem waiting inside.

Actually, I *did* reach a point at which, on occasion, I would remember to side-step the one in the entrance. And, on rarer occasions, to by-pass the back-up job in the kitchen. Though seldom on the same night. The one night I finally managed to accomplish this feat it was with no little arrogance that I strode into the living room—only to run into another brow-dimpler cleverly positioned on the direct route to the recliner chair. As this still left space on my noggin for at least one more good-sized lump, my wife abandoned all routine housework to concentrate on an arrangement for the bedroom.

Maybe two or three weeks later—it could have been months; I'd sort of lost track of time—she began to notice that I was now running the course with more glancing blows than those good old full-brow tooth rattlers. So her only alternative was to juggle their locations. One plant needed more light. Another, less draft. Another was too far from the radio to hear the music. Those were *her* excuses for the switcheroo. But I knew the real reason.

The one thing that kept me offering up my head for a gong was a stupid belief that her hobby by now had reached the end of its rope, so to speak. But coming home weary to the point of carelessness was to prove child play to coming home lit at night—make that late at night—when she has forgotten to leave a light on.

By coincidence, it's the nights I come home around 3 a.m. rather than the prescribed 11 p.m. that she forgets to clue me to the front door. On the occasion of this last 3 a.m. session, I had declined my buddy's offer to let me wear his hard hat home. I decided that a blow on the bare brow would be less destructive than having my head ricochet off one of those buckets of potting soil while cocooned in his inverted coal scuttle. Besides, I had a better idea, an idea that was going to get me from doorway to bed without having my bell rung, as they say in football.

I had drawn a map. A Macrame Map. And I had bought a penlight, guaranteed not to wake your wife when coming in at 3 a.m. Since this night I wouldn't be taking the scenic route over to the coffee table and down behind the sofa, I had limited my Captain Kidd masterpiece to a direct path from front door to bed.

You can imagine the restored confidence with which I approached our blacked-out front door with my penlight and map this particular night. If you can't, I'll tell you: It was with restored confidence. And it remained restored the whole time I was bent over trying to fit the key into the doorknob. Not until I recollected that the doorknob with the key slot was in our former house did I straighten up into the overhead bowling alley.

She had hung a new creation that day from the porch ceiling. I went down on all fours. I lost my penlight. My map blew away. I tore my slacks. And I hit all but one of those other antipersonnel booby traps getting to the bedroom—missing that one only because of still being on my hands and knees from the preceding one.

The next evening, I came home to find my wife out on the porch with miniature rake, hoe and shovel, happily bustling around a huge plastic ball perched atop this giant fluted pedestal. One half of the ball had been slid back and she was leveling a sack of potting soil across the inside.

Lost in curiosity, I completely forgot about her latest masterpiece with which I had tangled the night before. It was therefore with superb control that I managed to jest, "You'll never get it off the ground!"

"It's a terrarium," she trumpeted, the old gleam of anticipation lighting her big brown eyes.

So now I'm not so sure. If she *does* get that brute off the ground, I may take my buddy up on his hard hat offer. On second thought, I may go down to the marina and rent one of those deep-sea divers' helmets. At least until my head resumes its original noble shape.

Chapter 3

HAPPY FATHER'S *DAY*—

MOTHER AND KIDS

There's a movement afoot (and this is it) to have Father's Day changed from the month of June to the month of April. All Fool's Day would be appropriate, although any time before Mother's Day will do. It's Mother Day that leaves the kids teetering on the brink of bankruptcy. And it's dear old mom on whom they have shot their wad of sentiment for the year. One day out of 365 set aside, supposedly, to honor the old man—who himself is still making payments on his wife's Mother's Day gala—and the piggy banks are empty, the heart strings plucked to the drooping stage.

It was last year's spectacular, in which I was to be the designated centerpiece, that lent feet to this movement now afoot.

Kids who have fluttered from the nest develop their own subtle ways of letting pop know that just making it home for the big occasion is in itself a magnificent gesture.

Anything over and above this sacrifice of time and effort is pure extravagance.

Our son ran out of gas coming up the driveway. He then used my special tube for racking wine to siphon enough gas from my tank to get his car up to the house. I ran out of gas the next morning on my way to work.

With everyone accounted for, the big moment of "gift" presentation had arrived.

My kids' combined contribution, cleverly wrapped in a grocery sack slit along one side and tied with what looked to be dental floss, consisted of a genuine monkeypot horseshoe crab, all the more valuable, as was quickly pointed out, because the bottom and top didn't match. The envelop accompanying this prime candidate for the attic contained, to my daughter's embarrassment, an overdue telephone bill instead of a Father's Day card. This got a good laugh all around. Around to me, that is, as the bill included a 16-minute call from Indianapolis to Lubbock, Texas. In prime time.

In an effort to outdo me sentimental-wise for the sewing machine I had given her for Mother's Day, my dear wife went to heaven-only-knew-what expense to add to my treasures the cordless grass trimmers she had been wanting for the past two years. Heaven and I both knew at the end of the month, because I got the bill.

That's another thing. On *her* day, mother is always taken out to dinner, the vote going three to nothing, with one abstention, that she should be spared the labor of cooking. But has one of the three "yes" voters ever stepped forward or offered to arm wrestle me for the restaurant tab when it's presented? No. And no one in the group having yet come up with a subtle strategy for out-fumbling dear old dad for the bill on *his* day, the old man's mess is served at home.

They do make one concession for this weight-watcher's banquet: I am allowed to choose the menu. My choice hasn't varied since I first became a father: broiled ham steak and butterscotch pie. And that's pie made from scratch, not from pudding.

I have yet to get either.

Following the gift-unveiling ceremonies at this last tribute, I retired to the garden to hoe up an appetite befitting a feast of broiled ham steak and butterscotch pie. After our three-week drought, the soil could certainly use the saliva I would lose in fantasizing.

When my dear wife finally whanged the triangle (a surprise—shock, rather—Christmas gift the year I had requested a desk set) to call the gang to dinner, it was no surprise, the way things had been going, to find the menu completely devoid of broiled ham steak. And the butterscotch pie not only hadn't been made from scratch, it had been scratched altogether. By popular ballot, taken while I was outside the precinct working up an appetite, we would be dining on creamed tuna on toast.

"You can have broiled ham steak any old time," the cook consoled me. "But the kids didn't want to see me slaving over a hot broiler on a day like this."

"They could have looked the other way, then," I argued. "As long as you had the oven on for the butterscotch pie," I pointed out, hoping to humble her still further, "surely you could have tossed in a few ham steaks."

"That's something else..." she pointed back—the upshot being that, short of a Mother Fletcher pie truck tipping over in our front yard, there would be no butterscotch pie. A further poll of the members had come out with a preference for ice cream, with son magnanimously volunteering to drive into town to buy a quart (after siphoning more gas from my car to make the trip.) The vote, by four to zilch, had gone to chocolate. And I hate chocolate. But a flavor I hate I can eat a quart of without any help.

Entertainment for Mother's Day is never a problem. Mother likes to digest while father knots his stomach on a lovely bumper-to-bumper drive with five adults and two grandchildren brandishing lollipops donated by the restaurant cashier while dear old dad is shelling out $42.78 to settle the tab. When at long last the traffic thins out to where the drive is no longer exciting, then I can turn around and bumper-to-bumper back home again.

But what can the family do in the way of entertainment to make the day a memorable one for pop? Hand him a whittling stick and a sharp knife? Read to him from their collection of overdue bills and dunning letters? Or could they, just this one time, leave him alone to watch the three-hour coverage of the final round of the U.S. Open Golf Tournament (a Father's Day opportunity that occurs but once in a life time)?

I had no more than turned on the tube and settled down with my one-seventh of a quart of chocolate ice cream, when the family, by democratic process, legislated to have Dear Old Dad's Day commemorated by a junket to McCormick's Creek State Park.

"Come on," cried my dear wife, gaily prying my fingers loose from the sofa arm. "We'll be back in time for the final putt—and that's all that counts." Funny, I had never thought of that.

If I had to go, at least I'd drive. By rushing through the entertainment maybe I could manage to see the entire final hole, tee off and all. But no, this being *my* day, etiquette called for my son to do the driving—after another transfusion from my gas tank, needless to say.

The object that our son calls a car is a 1962 Buick convertible without benefit of muffler. This actually made little difference due to the volume control of his radio being stuck on "deafening." My intermittent protests that too much excitement from looking at the trees might be bad for my heart fell like cricket chirps in a rock-crushing plant. How we happened to make it home with two holes of the Open yet to be played, I owe to the rain and a rusty top that refused to go up.

That tournament, you'll recall, had been designed in Heaven especially for Father's Day. John Mahaffey was leading Jerry Pate by one stroke, with Al Geiberger and Tom Weiskoph only one stroke behind him. But no...the kids were not through entertaining me yet. I could watch "that stuff" and still finish off this gala with "one of our good old euchre games."

Consequently, I was playing a good old game of euchre at the time someone's ball went into the water on the 18th, with someone else hitting his second shot within two feet of the flag and then putting in for the win. What with all the yelling, of such things as, "Come on, Dad, it's your play!" and "Hey, Dad, you discarded the *right bower!*" I was lucky to hear the announcer scream that this was the most thrilling U.S. Open finish of all time. I read in the next morning's paper that it was Mahaffey's ball that went into the water and that

Jerry Pate had won his very first victory with an incredible birdie on the final hole.

After the girls had left, my son challenged me to one of our grand old games of chess. Taking it as a gesture of atonement, I nearly broke down. I recovered rather quickly, however, after he suggested putting "a little something on the game to make it interesting." What he had in mind turned out to be an IOU against enough gas from my tank to get home on. This cost me not only the gas (seems he had been reading a book on how to win at chess), but a movie I had wanted to watch on TV and two hours sleep.

I have already formulated plans for Mother's Day next year. In the meantime I hope the new administration in Washington will do something about legalizing a national day to honor kids. They're the ones I'm *really* out to get.

Maynard Good Stoddard

Chapter 4

ROADWAY ROULETTE

Husbands often become so self-centered they fail to recognize the many subtle ways in which their wives fill the void after the kids have flown the nest. I, in all modesty, am not one of them.

Most noticeable to me is the way my wife fills the void when we are traveling on one of those monotonous stretches of freeway.

I mean, without kids in the car, no more stopping at the first food exit after breakfast for something to munch on—anything to make stopping at the next two exits for drinks a necessity ... and for a rest room at the following two exits even more vital—not to mention emergency stops should those exits lie more than 10 miles apart.

To quit all this fun cold, of course, can give a man withdrawal symptoms of the worst kind.

But my wife, bless her heart, has filled the gap. Through the subtle development of an inventory of highway games, she now takes my mind off the monotony of freeway travel completely.

The game she seems to favor—at least it usually comes first in her repertoire—is the one I call "Heart Attack." The rules go like this:

The car must be a minimum of 10 miles from the starting point in heavy traffic, with the next exit a minimum of 10 miles ahead. She begins the game by suddenly clapping a hand to her forehead. She may at the same time mutter, "Oh, no," but this is optional.

As soon as she sees my heart fibrillating to the point of fluttering my necktie, she begins a frantic search of her pockets. Then a feverish inventory of her purse. Followed by a desperate ransacking of the glove compartment. And finally a last-hope check of the rear seat. If I have by this time pulled safely off onto the berm, she scores one point. If I have pulled off at a speed that sends the car plunging down an embankment, she is awarded three points. Rack up one point if the car is not totaled, three if we can both walk away.

In case of a tie, I win the game, if I can guess just what the heck it is she forgot. I lost the last one by guessing it *had* to be the deed to the Taj Mahal. A packet of Kleenex was the correct answer.

Her second selection is usually a game involving the heater in the winter, the air conditioner in summer. "Roastie Toastie," the heater contest, has proven the more exciting. My personal thermostat hovers around 17. My wife's hovers around three below. Thus the object here is for me to keep from stripping to the waist and for her to stay comfortable without wrapping up in a blanket.

The game usually doesn't begin until I get sleepy and open my window. Just a crack is plenty. At the first whiff of fresh air, she throws herself into the contest by turning the heater to High. I accidently turn it off altogether while dusting the speedometer with the end of my necktie. She begins hugging herself and *brrring* every couple of miles. When this fails to win the game, she reaches into the back seat for her sweater, making a big to-do of getting into it, as if maybe her arms were already too numb to function properly. But they usually function well enough that when her contortions finally subside, I find the heater back on High.

After my glasses begin to fog, I have no choice but to roll my window all the way down. She counters by grabbing her hair with both hands as if to keep it from being blown out by the roots. If I now roll the window back up, she wins. If I don't, and she can drape a scarf over her head and tie it under her chin in such a manner as to have passing motorists sympathizing over her case of mumps (or worse, fresh-air-fiend husband), I lose.

Games are often called on account of rain. Not hers. In fact, a few sprinkles of rain *make* one of her more exciting contests. That's all it takes for an excuse to reach over and flip on the windshield wipers. The object here is to smear bugs completely across my line of vision. If she can smear them so thickly that I am forced to pull off the highway ... (see scoring for Heart Attack game).

Some of these diversions—particularly the last one—are over before we know it. Her fun-filled "Why, Where and When to Stop," on the other hand, never fails to keep us entertained for hours.

She has, of course, several possibilities. If it isn't a restaurant it's a rest room. If not a rest room, a motel. If none of the three, it is what she calls "points of interest."

Our last point of interest, to give you an idea, was 55 miles off our route, cost $2.50 each for admission and consisted of a sick donkey, two goats, a garter snake, a bunch of mice and a row of empty cages bearing labels of Lion, Zebra, Aardvark, Polar Bear, Elephant and Wildebeest. For another buck each we were treated to the spectacle of the garter snake devouring a mouse, during which one of the goats seized the opportunity to run off with my wallet, which I had stashed in my hip pocket for safekeeping.

The thing that makes the What, Where and When game so lively is that I was born under the sign of the Camel. I can go for 500 miles without a drink. My wife, however, can't so much as see a Coke sign without her tongue swelling.

Maynard Good Stoddard

We must, therefore, contest every possible source of potables and, of course, every possible source of relief: rest area, welcome center, service station, bush—you name it. As for games going overtime; I have seen ten women go into a rest room *after* my wife and watched all ten come out before she showed up. Whether she's overly polite, forgets the dime and has to crawl under, or is bothered with some sort of condition, I am never in the mood to inquire.

Our stomachs, being no better synchronized, provide her with yet another source of highway high jinks.

I am hungry at lunchtime. She isn't. The reason I am hungry; I'm so eager to get started on the day's games that I seldom bother with more than doughnuts and coffee for breakfast. She believes she can't play her best on less than a hearty meal of pancakes and sausage. And while I spend the forenoon working up an appetite at the wheel, she confines her activity to the manipulating of the instrument panel gadgets and short walks to relief areas.

"Don't mind me," she says, to open the game. "Just because I'm not hungry is no reason for you not to take this ideal driving time to pull off the highway and look around for a restaurant. At least I can come in and get warm" (or cool off, depending on the season).

But how can a man go into a restaurant and eat while his wife sits across the table and watches, as though they had tossed a coin and he had won? I haven't figured it out. And she knows it. So I order a hamburger to go. I could easily eat two, but knowing that she will be hungry the minute we get back on the highway (which gives her a two-point bonus), I'll wait until we get off at the next exit.

"I had better hold that until we get started," she will unfailingly offer. And, "That does smell good," she will say, also without fail.

The way the scoring goes, if I am left with more than that part of the bun where the hamburger didn't reach, I get five points. I haven't scored five points yet. And with my hamburger now reposing in her stomach (three points), we won't be stopping again for another two hours ... unless bugs blot out my vision ... or she sees a Coke sign.

And then there are the possibilities for a rest stop.

Oh, what fun it is to ride...

Chapter 5

LOVE, HONOR AND REPAIR

Why is it that the married woman will replace her utility knife carefully in its protective wooden wall rack, return her pinking shears dutifully to their form-fitting box, insert her knitting needles patiently into their velvet-lined sheath, and then can go out and bank the power mower off the doghouse without batting an eye? Or leave the refrigerator door open until the motor begins to smoke? And then think nothing of firing up the furnace to defrost her eyebrows?

I can tell you why in one word: Husband.

You'll never find the single woman melting the wires on her toaster drying out a paper towel. Not unless there's a pushover handyman neighbor next door. When her movable parts stop moving or her burnoutable parts are burned out, it's up to her, of course, to do the repairing or else risk bankruptcy calling in a specialist or going in debt for new equipment. The married woman, on the other hand, has only to dump the problem into the lap of this jackass of all trades, whom she took for better or worse or lousy (in my particular case, when it comes to repair work, it's lousy), and blithely walk away. Her responsibility ends when the wires burn off or when the movable parts fail to move.

To borrow a favorite phrase from Henny Youngman: Take my wife, please.

Water for our country kitchen is brought from the cistern and forced through the taps by a pump located beneath the sink. To save the motor the struggle of starting up, I will shave in the water Lois has used for boiling eggs. Weather permitting, I take my Saturday night bath down at the creek, beating myself against a rock. She, on the other hand, will set the pump in labor for the sole purpose of wetting her bangs. Her reasoning is: Why run around with dry bangs when you've got a husband to keep the pump in repair?

It doesn't seem to matter what she's shortening the life of, as long as it's something that will have me scratching my head with greasy fingers when it expires.

I mean, she will get out the sweeper to suck a wisp of navel lint from the bedroom floor. I will spend the week after Christmas picking up artificial snow from the carpet by hand. She air-conditions the car or turns on the heater to drive to the mailbox. I *walk* to the mailbox—the entire length of the driveway. She turns up the thermostat to dry the panty hose she'll be wearing three days later. I dry my socks on my feet. When she hasn't been active enough to keep her self-winding watch wound, she sticks it in the blender. I can keep my watch wound just from wringing my hands in despair.

When it comes to shooting down the old man's weekend or getting him off the sofa in the evening, however, nothing can beat keeping the refrigerator motor running until it belches its last belch.

If I am opening the refrigerator door, I at least have a faint idea of what it is I am after. And often of where it is located. When I'm putting in instead of taking out, I jerk the door open, shove the stuff in, slam the door shut. So maybe I did get a little cole slaw in the Jell-O that time—it's not a bad combination. And those eggs had to be cracked some time anyway, as I pointed out during the subsequent inquisition.

Lois, true to her female heritage, is a browser. She opens the door and just stands there, sometimes humming in contentment. Not until she hears the old motor come to life does she get around to lifting the lid of a dish and maybe remarking, "That looks like cole slaw in the Jell-O!" Or she will begin to move things from one shelf to another. At other times she is satisfied just rearranging things on the same shelf. And then there are times when she will jump one dish over another, putting the jumped dish into the vegetable drawer, as if in a game of Refrigerator Checkers.

Now that she's sure the motor is smoking real good, she begins her space-saving routine by emptying each dish into a smaller dish. By the time she is finished the furnace has come on and she's back to just standing there, trying to remember what it was she was after in the first place.

As a general rule, the bigger the disaster the more dramatic can be the breaking of the news to hubby. But Lois, I'll give her credit (How can I deny her credit when not a single repair service in town has turned her down?), appears equally thrilled to be shortening the life of items down in the $10 to $30 range.

And another thing. When these movable or burnoutable parts are moving or still give juice, the item is *ours*. The minute the parts cease to produce, they become *yours*. And there is no joy like that of a woman calling the office:

"*Your* furnace just blew up!" "*Your* electric carving knife quit halfway through the curtain rod I was trying to shorten!" "I got only three walnuts cracked and now *your* ice crusher just sits there and whines!"

Only last week it was that *our* car became my personal property.

She had driven into town to buy a new belt for her sewing machine, the old belt having caught fire while she was sewing up a stuffed turkey. And I had no more than settled myself nicely on the sofa than she was on the phone with the exhilarating news that *"my* car wouldn't run." It had suffered a coughing spell and expired while she was trying to parallel park in front of the Singer shop. And what was I going to do about it?

Eight miles away, and with my automotive skills limited to the checking of the oil, I suggested that she, just this once, turn the problem over to the nearest service station mechanic.

As it turned out, *my* car had been out of gas.

Lois herself was in such a state of disrepair upon returning home that she immediately had to wet her bangs. This started the pump again. And to warn off pneumonia from those wet bangs, up went the thermostat, which started the furnace. Not taking any chances, after browsing through the refrigerator for a Mello Yello she turned the oven on Bake and sat down in front of the open door. Which started me for the creek.

Not that it was warm enough for a bath—I just felt like beating myself against a rock.

Chapter 6

FOR BETTER OR WORSE

Statistics showing marriage and divorce rates in this country running neck and neck may be startling to some—particularly the single people. And they may well be asking how come so many couples who voluntarily, in most cases, joined their plights in holy matrimony (or however that goes) are now taking their mates for worse rather than for better.

Well, my wife and I vulcanized our futures on Dec. 7, 1941. (Or was that the beginning of our war with Japan? I get the dates confused.) And, in all fairness, I can think of maybe one or two excuses I have given her for running back to her mother. Counterclockwise, I can also come up with a couple dozen reasons why I could be excused for running off to Rio with my secretary and the contents of the company cookie jar.

Take just a simple little example that occurred only a few days ago. I came back from town with a can of "Five Percent Sevin' to dust on my Crenshaw melons. Going into the bedroom to slip into my gardening clothes, I set the can of dusting powder on the vanity. My wife at the same time dashed in from her bath, late for an appointment. Could I help it if her can of body powder and my can of Sevin looked so much alike?

"Look at the bright side, dear," I said. "At least this season you won't be bothered with aphids, thrips, Japanese beetles or Mexican leafhoppers." I rattled off a number of other pests I had saved her from, but it didn't help. She still glares at me whenever she scratches, which is frequently.

Apart from singular episodes of this nature, there are three main reasons for divorce, the predominant one being marriage. The other two are money and sex, with sex now going under the guise of incompatibility. (Or, as in the bumper sticker, "There would be fewer divorces, if he had more income and she was more pattible.")

Divorce doesn't occur at the drop of a hat, or a pair of shoes at 3 o'clock in the morning when he was due home from bowling at 10 p.m. Nor is it the wife shooting 30 bucks for a bag of groceries she can carry home in her teeth or pleading headache on their anniversary night that causes a man to haul out his suitcase and yell, "Okay, Nora, I've had it!" The crumbling marriage (and you might want to write this down, in case your old high school should ask you for a motto to inscribe across the front of the new gym), the crumbling marriage, I say, is built upon the grains of quicksand accumulated over the years of attrition from the irresistible male ego confronted by the immovable female logic, watered periodically by the tears of the latter.

Mixed in, of course, we find those innocent remarks a husband may make, often in jest, often in haste, often while under the influence, but always tucked away in the memory bank of you-know-who.

In a brief brouhaha one night at a night club I excitedly yelled at an overly ardent inebriate, "Take your hands off my filthy wife!" She has remembered it.

The invitation to our company picnic read, "Bring your own tableware and one hot dish." I said I would take my secretary. She has remembered it.

I once remarked to our preacher that I was content with the simple things in life, and included my wife in the list. She has remembered it.

There is also the tender subject of cooking. The eternal question being, Does a woman's cooking improve or does a husband just get conditioned to it? Some men don't want to find out. Most suffer in silence and hope for the best. A few add to the divorce rate by having the courage to speak out.

One brave man complained that after three years he was still getting pitch-in meals—one taste and he pitched them in the sink. He was the same fellow who announced he was buying his wife a pair of safety shoes to wear in the kitchen when she baked biscuits. Another one stated that no one could cook like his wife, but the Army came close. He also claimed that natives came clear from Africa just to dip their arrows in her chili. A third now-single chap tried to coax his wife to write a cookbook entitled, *"Kamikaza Kooking."* These boys were bucking not only for a divorce but for a transfusion as well.

The nearest I have ever come to taking exception to my wife's kitchen caprices was the night I asked her how come the dishes the dog licked came out cleaner than the ones she did. "Because the dog has a bigger tongue!" she snapped. And when my wife snaps, it's best not to pursue the subject further.

I have noticed—and this is just between us—that a woman tends to cook what *she* likes to eat. My wife likes to eat bacon and tomato sandwiches at least four times a week. Worse, since the price of a pound of bacon is now about what a farmer used to get for a whole hog, she makes a sandwich from a single strip. I have to keep peeking in and moving the bacon forward or the sandwich is over. Unless I want to eat a plain tomato sandwich, which isn't my favorite. But there are too many other irritations to dwell on this one.

My wife being a nurse and thus in the habit of waking patients to give them a sleeping pill, takes morbid delight in waking me on the sofa and telling me it's time to go to bed. Or, let me be lying there in transcendental meditation before retiring, and she will lay aside her needlepoint, as she did the other night, and out of the blue say, "Do you want to be buried with your glasses on or off?" Sleep is no problem after that—it just can't be done.

Then there is woman's favorite recreation—talking. If John Cameron Swayze wants to put the Timex to a real test, he should tape it to a woman's lower lip. An Oklahoma weatherman once reported his wife could talk 142 words a minute, with gusts up to 180. I haven't timed my wife's rate, but it's enough at times to make my ears smart. Not that she and I don't have words. It's just that I don't have a chance to use mine. Whenever we sit down to have a long talk, she has the long talk, I have a long listen.

Traditionally, a woman is supposed to object to her husband reading the paper at breakfast. My woman prefers it. It eliminates possible oral competition. If I get her to take some of the paper, she reads to me from her section. Thus I keep pretty well informed on white sales, women's fashions and who did what to whom in Ann Landers. But if I want to know which team is leading the American League, I have to ask a boy on a vacant lot (please don't ask me how come a lot is vacant if there's a boy on it).

Another thing, when I do manage to get in a word, it's so edgewise as to be unrecognizable or such a novelty that she pays no attention. The last time I got one in she looked up from her box of chocolate-covered cherries and said,. "What were you saying about Dow Jones' earned run average?"

Some wives have curves, most have angles. When mine wants something, or wants to do something which she knows I am too sensible to agree to, she merely broaches the subject and then sits back and lets it ferment in the little wooden keg on my shoulders. She knows it won't be long before I begin thinking it is *my* idea and we'll go ahead with it.

Example: She wanted to go to Hawaii for our umptyfifth anniversary. I wanted to go to McCormick's Creek Park for a weenie roast. The closer it got to Dec. 7 or whatever the date, the clearer I could hear ukulele music and the roar of the surf, not to mention the rustle of grass skirts. (And I didn't mention it, for good reason: One night I put my foot down and bravely announced that I was going to Shannon's Roaring Twenties or know the reason why. And she picked my foot up and told me the reason why.) Anyway, instead of spending about $2.50 for hot dogs and buns and maybe another buck for gas, we shot $1,600 on a trip to Hawaii. It was the most expensive idea I ever had.

Because I believe in writing only on subjects I know a little something about, I am leaving the sex problems in divorce to the sexpert—Dr. David Reuben, Masters and Johnson, Harold Robbins, Hugh Hefner and that crowd. But when it comes to money, or the lack thereof, I pride myself on being somewhat of an authority. And, thanks to inflation, I become more authoritative by the day.

The zodiac aside, normal women are born under the dollar sign. Their main mission in life is to spend. And normal women pursue this sacred responsibility with a zeal that would rank Carrie Nation and Florence Nightingale as campfire girls by comparison.

My wife can spend money faster than anyone. She is so well known at local stores that any day she doesn't show up the managers telephone to see if she's sick. The one time I trusted her with a $20 bill to "run to the grocery for a loaf of bread," she ran back with $20 worth of groceries. She has a Teflon billfold (nothing will stick to it). If they only had competition at the state fair in getting rid of money, she would have enough blue ribbons by now to make a quilt. I sometimes think she believes that all money was printed by lepers. Or perhaps as a child she struck a corner of her head on a cash register and she is devoting her life to getting even.

My one hope, now that I have been brainwashed to where I'll never be a statistic in the divorce column, is that Ralph Nader may read this piece. If he does, the 1941 (or whatever that date) wives may be recalled. In which case I will require a loaner until mine comes back from the shop. The more I think of it, that could very well be the solution to the whole divorce problem.

Chapter 7

BED ETIQUETTE

Good bed manners begin prior to the act of jumping into bed. They begin by informing the husband, who'll be coming home late, that the main items of bedroom furniture will be transposed by the time he hits the old sack—or the spot where the old sack used to be.

As a case in point, I crept into our house late one night after an exhausting day of selling ladies' unmentionables (which, for several years, I forced myself to mention) door to door. So as not to wake my dear wife (who was at that moment chewing on her pillow to keep from snickering and spoiling the show), I climbed the stairs in my sock feet, undressed in the dark, walked over and dropped onto what should have been the bed. Only it wasn't the bed. It was the vanity. Bottles flew, vials broke, jars rolled, atomizers atomized, and for the next week, I smelled like an Avon lady direct from a three-day tour of the factory. As for getting all the glass out of my nether anatomy, the project still hasn't been completed.

The right to snore, especially after a hard day's work selling feminine underpinning, is my candidate for the Fifth Freedom. There are those who hold, however, that snoring is more a candidate for grounds of incompatibility. And hold further that any and all means of putting an end to that "unholy racket" is justified.

Proper etiquette, of course, calls for the snoree to shake the snorer gently by the shoulder and murmur lovingly, "You're at it again, dear." But there are snorees who resolve the first offense of the night by kneeing the snorer in the kidneys with such authority that he doesn't get at it again for the next two hours. Offense number two has been known to end with an attempt on the snorer's life via pillow over his face or, at best, a crude invitation to knock it off or spend the rest of the night on the couch. One hears rumors that a third offense is sometimes terminated by the clamping of a clothespin over the nose of the offender. Fortunately, I've never been able to get back to sleep after offense number two.

Another bedtime barbarism that could stand a little etiquette concerns the temperature of the sleeping partner's feet. Why the female foot drops to 20 below the minute she hits the bed, while the male foot remains its own warm, pleasant self, is probably a difference in genes, hormones, calories, the id—stuff like that. Or maybe it's just nature's way of saying, "Not tonight, Buster." Then again, it could be that she leaves one of her feet hanging outside the covers until frost forms, suffering the discomfort for the sheer pleasure of ramming it into her sleeping opponent's back. I suppose, in all fairness, there *is* some sport in watching old semisleeping hubby suddenly shoot up over the headboard and roll off into the nightstand.

That's another thing. In going to bed, as in going through doors and into elevators, I'm still old-fashioned enough to let my wife precede me. Of course, if the bed happens to be warmed up when I arrive, so much the better. However, once her posterior, her eight arms and the foot that hasn't been left outside to chill have staked out her claim, it's a toss-up whether I'll spend the night clinging to my edge of the bed or join the flea motel we call a dog on the floor. Rather than hang around waiting for her to have a subconscious relapse and move over, I have tried getting up, walking around and sliding in on her other side. But that leg leading to the foot being iced is a bother.

Bed etiquette, in other words, was never more urgently needed than during the winter season. Especially for anyone having an allergy to cold sheets, And more especially for anyone intimidated by the first menacing growl after finally getting up the nerve to encroach upon a preheated area. Thus I, for one of those anyones, am nightly required to turn my hemoglobin up to High and warm as best I can my own little corner of the percales.

And how patiently my dear wife waits—waits for my knees finally to pull away from my stomach and my feet to begin inching downward. At this signal that the top sheet covering me may now be warmer than the top sheet covering her, it's time to turn over and take the top sheet with her, leaving me to warm up the next section from scratch.

I really haven't checked, but by the number of times she can do this in the span of one night, this clever little woman has arranged our top sheet to operate on the principle of the roller towel. And any attempt to reverse the thing is useless. Anyone clever enough to come up with the idea is clever enough to install a stop-lock.

Not to rattle the skeleton in the family closet, or however that goes, but I occupy a bed with a woman who has what is known in medical circles as "Restless Legs." Vicious would be a more accurate adjective. What they do, as regular as Old Faithful, is lash out, toenails at the ready, every minute and 12 seconds. I could set the alarm clock by it. On occasion, when the toenails have found their mark and are anchored in the calf of the other occupant's legs, they may miss an eruption. But by this time, said other occupant is usually headed for the medicine cabinet.

Maynard Good Stoddard

My suggested solutions have fallen upon the ear turned toward the pillow. The night she must have been dreaming of pedaling up the Matterhorn on a rusty bicycle, I hinted at installing a bundling board. Just a little something about three feet high that would limit my nightly pain to an occasional splinter and possibly spare me the unpleasantness of a series of rabies shots. She wasn't for it. The thermal socks I gave her, thinking they might dull the bite of her toenails, she is wearing in her outdoor boots. And the long sheath nightgown, which I hoped would serve as a hobble, she is saving for good.

Speaking of sheath nightgowns, that's another little matter. Perhaps not of national urgency, but it pertains to those occasions when hubby comes home lit (excuse me, late) from a night out with the "boys." Rules of etiquette call for the night light to be on, his side of the bed turned down and his worried wife waiting to receive him with a deep sigh of relief that he has once again returned safely to her tender loving arms. The occasion of one of my recent (meaning within the past five years) nights out proves, however, that the rules are not always followed to the letter.

Once I had stumbled my way into the bedroom and fumbled my way into bed, my only intention, honestly, was to do the husbandly thing and offer my wife a friendly goodnight pat somewhere upon her person. But I couldn't find her person. Found her outline with no trouble, but I couldn't get to her, if you know what I mean. Reaching down to where her nightgown should have ended, it didn't. At the risk of smothering, I worked my way down to the foot of the bed and still hadn't come to the end of it. She, in fact, had gone to all the trouble of tucking the bottom of her nightgown under the mattress. The old headache route would have been more subtle, I thought to myself (having always had trouble thinking to someone else.) And while I was still down there trying to figure the thing out, one of her restless legs erupted and caught me squarely on the chin.

The next morning, while trying to ingest my oatmeal through a straw, my dear wife said, "How come you slept on the top sheet last night?"

Although now too late to do me any good, still my love for my fellow man compels me to recommend that rules governing bed etiquette be made a part of the ceremony that troughs a couple's plights. "Do you, Kitty Crumcake, promise to love, cherish, surrender half the bed, keep your cold feet to yourself..." and so on. Then, hopefully, some of these sleeping contingencies would stop continging. And a man might occasionally get a good night's sleep, instead of having to grab what he could at his desk the next day.

Chapter 8

ALL THINGS SICK AND SORROWFUL

"Can you come home right away!" my wife shrilled over the phone. "The cat's got a fishhook in her nose!"

Dropping my dictation notes and my secretary, I made the wild three-mile dash from the office to our house.

Sure enough, the lousy cat, perhaps enticed by odors still emanating from my fishing gear stored overhead in the garage, had somehow managed to get its septum impaled by a fishhook and had come to the house trailing about 20 feet of eight-pound-test nylon line. Shari, our 80-pound daughter with a 70-pound heart, whose cat it was, was running around with her hands over her eyes and bumping into things. Lois, her mother—my wife, on the kids' side of the family—was running around yelling things like, "Do something!" "What are you going to do?" "Oh, the poor thing!" And "Watch out for the refrigerator!"

While she was putting cold compresses on Shari's head (the portion that had struck the refrigerator), I located a pair of wire cutters, skillfully snipped off the barb and withdrew the hook. But all the time I was reflecting on where I had gone wrong.

And what I reflected was, if only I had removed this flea motel from the doll buggy when I came home from work that first night, stripped it of its dolly dress, exiled the "precious little lost waif" to the alley from whence Shari had rescued it and laid down a rule governing pets, today I might be a well-to-do man, with blood pressure right on the 20/20 mark and my hair more pepper than salt. But I didn't, and I'm not, and they aren't.

Once the cat's adoption had been confirmed by a box of flea powder and a month's supply of store-bought cat food, Shari must have circulated a flier: "Give me your tired, your poor, your injured, your victims of broken homes yearning to be free...my dad's a pushover...pass it on."

First to test the validity of this open invitation was a pigeon sporting a wing that had been aerated by a BB gun. Lois, a registered nurse, answered the call of duty by postponing dinner to tweeze out the BBs and try to keep the patient breathing, or whatever it is birds do to stay alive.

After several days of Epsom-salt baths, hourly oatmeal-and-warm-milk feedings and half-hourly rescues from the jaws of the cat, "Pidgy" repaid the hospitality by flying off downtown, presumably to get himself shot professionally by one of the city-sanctioned sportsmen staked out on an off ice-building roof.

To fill the void, Shari's mother immediately sponsored her participation in the pet craze currently sweeping the neighborhood—the endearing hamster. Not a sensible single hamster. Oh, no. It had to be a stupid pair.

You can tell the sex of a parrot, so I've heard, by offering a piece of bacon. If he picks it up, it's a male; if she picks it up, it's a female. Unfortunately, salesgirls in dollar stores (formerly dime stores) have no such foolproof system for determining the sex of hamsters. So we, of course, got one of each gender.

And guess whose hamster hussy got herself in an interesting condition within five minutes after hitting our front door? You got it.

Something like five days later, the distressing event (which would continue on a regular schedule, I was joyously informed) was not, however, without its tragedy. The mother (I'll try to continue) died in hamsterbirth, leaving a family of six. That's not counting the suspected father, who alleviated his grief by taking a spin on the $7.98 exercise wheel inside the $19.95 cage.

Once more, Shari trustingly turned to her mother to keep the litter from joining *their* mother in that big hamster colony in the sky.

Having been assigned the emergency run to the shopping mall for a can of Karo syrup, a carton of enriched milk, an eyedropper and a bottle of rubbing alcohol, I got news of the *coup de grace* second hand. What happened, as nearly as I could make out in all the commotion, was that trustworthy Nurse Stoddard, to keep the little rascals warm, had arranged their bodies (but I get ahead of myself) on a pie plate and stuck them in the oven. Unfortunately, our oven is one off the older models without a hamster setting, and when the nurse looked in to check on the state of their health, they didn't have any. Done to a turn, as the saying goes. I arrived to find Shari running around with her hands over her eyes and bumping into things.

Shari and her remorseful mother came home from a sidewalk sale the next day with a pup. The last of the litter, they said. I believed them. Like many dogs in starting out, she was only a puppy, but she wasn't fooling me for a minute. The little beast already had feet the size of blackboard erasers and enough extra hide to cover a recliner. Within months, under the pretext of being glad to see me home, she would place those blackboard erasers on my shoulders and knock me over backwards,

"If we lived in the country," said Lois one night when she was helping me up and gathering the papers from my brief case, "the dog would be getting her exercise chasing rabbits and things. And she would practically live off the land."

NOTHING SERIOUS, I HOPE

That's how come I let myself be talked into buying these 13 acres of sandstone and clay here in Sweet Owen County, Indiana.

Three weeks after we moved in, Shari convinced me that the reason our place didn't compare with the neighbors' was because we didn't have a "brush goat." "Everyone has one," she lied, "to clean up the sassafras, wild grapes, wild onions and poison ivy." So I laid out $45 for a brush goat, so called.

Due to a lack of communications, however, the goat immediately began cleaning up the grapes in the arbor, the dwarf fruit trees, the berry bushes, the flower beds and the clothes off the line. And instead of having to be alert for blackboard erasers on my shoulders, now I can't bend over without running the risk of being butted into the middle of next week. He's just being playful, I am gleefully reminded.

After a few games of this, I let myself be talked into adding two "darling miniature donkeys" to the menagerie. They would not only play with the goat, but they thrive on sassafras, wild grapes, wild onions and poison ivy. Ours eat nothing but hay and oats in winter, and in summer, to reach the greener grass on the other side, knock down line fences faster than a city-bred man can put them back up. And in their haste, they don't mind stepping on a neighbor's lamb. Our neighbor was good enough to let us make restitution by buying it for about three times what it was worth.

Until the lamb's $44.60 cast comes off its right leg, Shari is keeping it in the root cellar. For physical therapy, the dog helps out by making daily attempts on its life. These sessions also have served to clear the lower shelves of all empty fruit jars.

As for the dog living off the land, this is as close as she has come. Whether it's the stimulating exercise, the invigorating country air or a shortage of moose in Owen County, we are now buying canned dog food by the case and dry dog food by the 50-pound sack. In gratitude, she has dug for moles until our front lawn could be turned into a clay tennis court without much effort. She keeps our garden and flower beds mulched with crow carcasses, cow skulls, chicken wings and selected chunks of debris from the trash burner. Although she had done her best to keep the hens (developed from those "sweet little baby chicks" the store had left over from Easter) out of the garden, to date she has managed to kill only three.

But things could be worse. And they are.

Going by the number of male callers lately, our dog must be a shoo-in for the title of Miss Congeniality of Owen County. My nights are now devoted mainly to discouraging the most ardent admirers from voting for her. The remainder of my nights go toward divesting my pajamas of cockleburs and my toes of thistles.

Keeping her shut in at night is like trying to sleep in the center cage at the dog pound. Tying her to the picnic table and leaving the porch light on is no improvement. This not only cost me a new picnic table but a trash burner as well, the old one being wiped out by the picnic table when she made her mad dash to welcome a timid caller.

To be honest, an 80-pound daughter with a 70-pound heart has its compensations. Our latest batch of kittens really is cute. And sometimes they get the attention of the puppies away from chewing on the rug. The dog finally has gotten down to business about digging the woodchuck out from under the house, and I'm using the dirt to fill in the holes made by the donkeys in their attempts to break the lamb's other leg when Shari brings it up for an airing. The pony with stringhalt that Shari said would be a steadying influence on the donkeys, come to find out, is not mean, as I first thought. His attempts to bite off my ear when I feed him, she says, are simply a sign of affection. He must love me dearly.

One of my city friends asked me the other day what we did for excitement in our little town of Freedom. Well, at the moment, the brush goat is headed for the woods with my pants that were drying on the line after I'd gone into the pond to rescue the lamb that had fallen off the old picnic table that Shari was using as a raft to give him some R & R. My credit cards and the car keys are in the pockets.

That should pretty well answer his question.

Chapter 9

THE TROUBLE WITH ZIPPERS

It's not that I won't be darkening the doors of a church again. It's just that I won't be darkening the door of Lawrence United Methodist on North Shadeland again. At least not until I grow a full beard to hide behind or the current generation of Lawrence Methodists dies off, whichever comes first.

Most of life's little deviltries I have come to accept. I mean, like standing on a street corner minding my own business and having a myopic wolfhound mistake my leg for a hydrant. I mean, passing out after giving blood at the blood bank and having to pay for a transfusion to get it back again. I mean, stopping at a nearly deserted Dairy Queen for a small-sized, unadorned cone and having a busload of schoolkids, half of them riddled with tapeworm, beat me to the counter.

Ergo, the situation last Sunday should have come as no surprise, for neither have I had what you might call a good rapport with things of a mechanical nature. I am the one who charges into the automatic door at the A&P lugging two sacks of groceries in each arm at the precise moment that a cinder flies into the electronic eye and the door doesn't pop open. And I ram the first four inches of my nose into the glass, totaling a carton of eggs, four light bulbs and the watermelon before the door recovers and sends me reeling into the parking lot.

I am the one whose key slides off the sardine can two inches from the starting tab, and I am required to pull the little fellers out with a buttonhook.

You know those "twist-off" caps on soft-drink bottles? I always cut myself. I can never open my *Reader's Digest Condensed Book* without a nail file, a pair of pliers and my wife—who finally does it for me.

Of the endless modern devices designed to unhinge people of my limitations, however, zippers and I are least congenial. I seldom get my coat liner zipped in until Christmas because all my spare time since October has been spent trying to get the mesher and the meshee into proper conjunction. I consistently manage to get my unsuspecting flesh caught in a zipper's vicious little teeth. And it is the zipper that often brings my wife and me to fighting pitch on evenings of formal occasions—with me trying to "zip her up" and her blousing over the zipper track and making guttural sounds until I yell at her to hold still, for Pete's sake, or we'll be there all night, and her sniffling that we *have* been there all night for two straight months, and we never go anywhere, and if I can't get her zipped up she'll call the plumber. (She calls the plumber when the car won't start. She says he can do everything. And from what we've paid him, he has.)

Anyway, there has been no love lost between zippers and me. But when they continue their caprices even on the Sabbath—and Communion Sabbath of *all* Sabbaths—I say it's time we went back to safety pins and binder twine.

My wife and I try to be early to church. Not only does this establish the impression that we are eager beavers, it also allows us to grab our favorite seats—last row, aisle. This vantage point, in turn, enables us to beat the crowd to Laughner's Cafeteria.

This being Communion Sunday, the ushers began ushing the congregation to the altar two pews at a time, beginning at the front. As is her custom Lois, the woman I had taken for better, waited until the usher had reached the row in front of us before plunging suddenly into her purse. Whether she was after a tissue, a Cloret, a run-stop for her pantyhose or her calorie counter, I've never been in the mood to inquire. But in zipping shut this pink-flowered clutch purse she managed to catch the edge of my brand new pink-and-white-striped jacket in the cogs. Not content merely to catch it, she then proceeded to grind it in past all redemption.

By the time the rest of the members of our row were on their feet, our combined efforts had succeeded in freeing the fabric from but one gear, with the death grip of at least five more still to be broken. And we were by now attracting glares that could loosely be translated as, "What are you, some kind of pagans?"

"Turn your coat up over it," hissed Lois, "and I'll walk close to you."

So, holding the side panel of my brand new jacket over the purse with my left arm, which I devoutly prayed would give the impression of nothing more untoward than a slipped truss, my dear wife and I labored down the aisle.

Immodestly nestled together as we were, the usher directing traffic at the altar riveted us with a look more often employed for Mr. & Mrs. Smith registering at a motel at 2 a.m. without luggage. Or maybe he thought I was trying to smuggle in a bottle of homemade wine. Whatever, he went to elaborate pains to break us up, directing Lois to the left, me to the right. I went to equal pains to make certain my jacket flap didn't flop down and satisfy his curiosity.

With both arms now committed, I could see no way of kneeling short of breaking both kneecaps. But after all, God has allotted man but one set of kneecaps. And I decided a soul will heal faster. So I reached out for the altar rail, my pink-and-white-stripped jacket flap dropped, the pink-flowered purse swung down and, my luck still holding, bounced off the shoulder of the loudest mouth in our church. Although I had never formally met the woman (and certainly have no intention of doing so), rumor has it that when it comes to disseminating the news, she is more colorful than Dan Rather and more dependable than the postal service. It would have come as no surprise had she left the altar early to begin spreading word that the church was harboring "one of those."

NOTHING SERIOUS, I HOPE

In times of stress I have always found solace in turning my thoughts to situations in which someone has experienced emotional upheavals of a similar nature. In this case I recalled the young chap having dinner at the country club with his girl friend and her parents, whom he was meeting for the first time. Everything had gone swimmingly until, upon retrieving his napkin from the floor, he happened to discover his fly brazenly agape. Surreptitiously laboring throughout the rest of the meal he managed to close the gap to a respectable dimension, but failed to notice that in doing so he had tucked in the tablecloth instead of his shirttail. Attempting to recover his cool by jumping up and asking his girl friend to dance, he had succeeded in pulling tablecloth, dishes, silver and the old man's after-dinner cigar onto the floor. It was reported that he dashed directly into the night, still dragging the tablecloth, seeking the nearest monastery recruiting station.

I would have preferred to be right behind him. As it was, if ever I am called upon the celestial carpet for taking Communion in my shirt sleeves and slipping out the side door instead of returning to our pew, I hope the heavenly accountant also noted that, even with the early start, I didn't try to beat the others to Laughner's. Even after my dear wife argued that she had seen other men eating there without a jacket.

But that wasn't the reason. The reason was, due to circumstances beyond my control, money for the dinner would have had to come from her pink-flowered clutch purse. And by the time I got rid of the thing, Laughner's was closed.

Chapter 10

KNIT 2, PURL 1, HUBBY 0

I am not what you could call a strong supporter of wife abuse. But when it comes to your basic marital noncompatabilities, I would pit husband neglect against wife abuse any old day. While a bruised ego may not stand out like a black eye in a divorce court, the wound is there, nonetheless, and lasts even longer.

What I mostly have in mind are those quiet evenings at home, man and wife, alone, together. With cares that infested the day behind them, these are the golden hours reserved for the scraping of barnacles off the great barrier reef of marriage. This is the pause in the day's occupation when he should be languishing on the sofa, his weary head resting comfortably on her lap, she contentedly stroking his brow or massaging his sagging shoulders after his tiring day on the golf course.

Instead, in the case with which I am most familiar, the wife no sooner sits than she immediately fortifies her lap and environs with one or more balls of yarn implanted with a menacing battery of knitting needles. Or she has a 10-foot bureau runner under construction as an excuse for jabbing out with her lethal crochet hook.

If this particular woman has managed to knit or crochet everything she can dream up at the moment—we have the only knitted dog blanket and crocheted mailbox cover in the neighborhood—she calls on the equally effective dodges of tatting, needlepoint, macrame, mattress stuffing, quilting—you name it. What it is isn't important just so long as it offers a reason for ignoring the man she once pledged to comfort, console, soothe, succor, sustain and otherwise attend to until death did them part. She contends that the vow automatically becomes null and void whenever the possible rusting of her knitting needles or crochet hook is at stake.

Early on, in the innocence of young husbandry, I spent many an evening risking permanent injury to my spine by sitting on the floor beside the dog, hoping that in a careless moment she might give me a pat on the head intended for him. It never happened. The closest those evening hours alone ever brought us to genuine husband-and-wifery was the night she used my ears to wind off a skein of yarn.

NOTHING SERIOUS, I HOPE

- Along in midwinter this year, I had every reason to believe that the situation might improve. Snowed in for two weeks, she finally ran out of yarn, string, thread, lint, hair—the works. The inconvenience of having our diet eventually reduced to parsnips and raspberry jam in no way compares to running completely out of idle-hour makin's. And even if she'd had the makin's, there wasn't so much as a doily left in the house that could have supported another row or whatever it is she does to them, the smallest already measuring at least two feet in diameter. Only a junkie needing a fix or a Girl Scout with a customer and no cookies could appreciate her dilemma. Her only avenue left to kill those dinner-to-bedtime hours lay in recognizing again that dear old hubby, quoting the Good Book, was still numbered among the quick.

In desperation, under the pretext that a thread near the center had been put in antigodkin, she began raveling her 12-foot crocheted tablecloth. Then she crocheted it back to its original condition. This required the better part of two evenings. When that woman begins purling and dropping, neither rain nor sleet nor dark of husband can keep her from her appointed rounds. Had it not been for a flare-up of arthritis in her purling finger, she might well have wrapped up the project in a single sitting.

How is it, I once asked myself, removing a cobweb suspended between my right ear and the sofa arm, that a woman who can't read the simple directions for changing a tire pasted inside the trunk lid has no trouble comprehending the hieroglyphic directions for constructing one of these knitted, knotted, needled or hooked masterpieces?

I had climbed from the floor to the sofa one night, under the delusion that I might get lucky enough to maneuver my head between a shuttling elbow and a crochet hook, when I was intercepted by the casual remark, "For Pete's sake, if you'd learn to do something like this instead of just lopping around, maybe my crochet hook wouldn't keep running up your nose! The directions are all right here." And she handed me this booklet, "Knitted and Crocheted Afghans."

How she had managed to learn Afghan I don't know (she went only one year to Michigan State), but I question if even an Afghan native could make head or tail of this stuff:

"Work .1 s c in each s c across side to center s c of 3 s

c at point, *3 s c in center s C, 1 s c in each of the next 9

s c, dec 2 sts in next s c (to dec: pull up a loop in each of *the next 3 sts, yo and pull through all loops at one time), 1*

*s c in each of the next s c, repeat from * once, 3 s c in*

next center s c, then complete opposite side in same manner.

Work 3 more strips in same manner."

Anyway, you think an expectant father is a nervous wreck? He can't hold a candle to a snowed-in woman faced with the prospect of hubby fawning at her feet and no barrage of needles protruding from a ball of yarn to keep his head at bay.

But I'll give this one woman credit. She came through without a dent in her record. At the critical moment, donning longjohns, mackinaw and boots, she wallowed down to the barn and came back with an armload of binder twine from the baled hay we had bought to feed the miniature ponies, her former hobby. (But ponies offer little excuse for the neglect of hubby in the evening, so hubby had inherited her hobby.) She spent the evening contentedly making hammocks for cast-iron flowerpots to be hung from the ceilings—and at a height carefully surveyed to greet a six-foot man just below the hairline.

The result proved to be so entertaining that she devoted the rest of her confinement to full-scale production. By the time a snowplow showed up, my once beautifully sculptured head had again assumed the baroque contour of the Hubbard squash.

Our snowy siege ended, she left immediately for town to "get something to do."

In fact, she just now staggered in. The box she's staggering under bears a picture on the side, under which, in depressingly large letters, is printed: "9- x 12-foot hooked rug."

And there go the next two years. At least.

Chapter 11

MY WIFE—AND OTHER GARDEN PESTS

"Did you read that piece in the Sunday *Star?*" my wife yelled over to me, leaning on the pickax she was using to loosen the so-called soil around our newborn pumpkin vines.

I shut off the Black & Decker drill I had extension-corded into the garden to make holes for a second planting of peas. "Could you narrow it down to the section of the paper it was in?" I called back.

"You know, about force-feeding milk to your vines. It said they would grow like crazy."

Coddle pumpkin vines with milk! True, the topsoil from our hilltop acreage here in Freedom, (Indiana, that is) has been reposing no doubt comfortably in the valley since shortly after God created the heavens and the earth. True, also, this left the top stratum 100 percent clay. And not just your plain old patty-cake clay. This was the type of clay from which billiard balls must be made. But, as any male gardener knows, where it might make a little sense to give the more refined cucumber or even muskmelon vine a booster shot of milk now and then, the pumpkin is a natural-born extrovert as it is."

"They don't require any milk," I called over to her. "Those things can germinate on a rock pile and be crossing Highway 67 a week later without any encouragement."

"I'd just like to try it on one," said she with her usual persistence.

"I'll have to sleep on it," said I, turning on my drill and going back to gardening.

And sleep on it I did. That very night, in fact...

My wife was in the garden with a quart syringe delivering a milk hypo to the vine she had selected as a guinea pig. After the second feeding, she hung a gallon jug from the shoulder of the scarecrow and began intravenous injections. All she could babble about was her upcoming blue ribbon for having the biggest pumpkin at the Owen County Fair.

By the time the jug went dry, the vine, now going under the name of Rover, had already roved ruthlessly over two rows of struggling beets, topped two rows of carrots, wiped out 10 feet of radishes, decapitated three artichokes, toppled six tomato plants, stakes and all, and, like the final linking of the Continental Railroad, had meshed calyxes with a butternut squash from the opposite end of the garden. (I had heard that cross-pollination went on, but I'd never been able to catch the little devils at it. I could only hope the neighbors wouldn't find out.)

Anyway, no sooner had I smashed the intravenous jug than my wife came out with a packet of sunflower seeds and made the mistake of asking, "Where should I stick these?"

Well, one thing led to another, and she ended up going back to the house. Later, when I felt this tickling on the seat of my pants, I thought, of course, it was her old ploy for patching things up. But it was Rover. Yes sir, that rascal had taken advantage of the argument to creep up my pants leg. I wished later I had thought to time myself; I could have been in the *Guinness Book of World Records* for fastest time in getting out of a pair of pants. My time in getting from the garden to concealment on the back porch wasn't bad either.

That night, for some reason, I couldn't sleep. And I didn't learn the reason until after midnight. Stamens flattened against our bedroom window, leaves trembling in frustration, anthers tapping impatiently on the window sill, there was Rover. I woke my wife and told her her pumpkin vine wanted his two o'clock feeding. She just groaned something about "stupid" and went back to sleep. This left it up to me to get out of bed, stumble to the refrigerator, fill a dishpan with milk and set it out on the patio. And I watched until Rover came creeping around the corner of the house and slurruped the whole thing. Didn't leave enough for our morning coffee.

The following evening began as one of those idyllic man-and-wife-at-home types: eating, loafing, reading, listening. The only snake in our little Eden was a box of milk chocolates lying invitingly on the coffee table. After maybe the fourth rustling of the box lid I said to my wife, "Don't you think you'd had enough candy?"

"Whadya mean *me!*" she said, "I thought it was you."

So I kept peeking over the top of my *U.S. News & World Report.* And, sure enough, Rover who had pushed out a window screen and worked his way under the rug to the sofa, came up the leg of the coffee table and ran his fat pedicel up under the box top to snitch a milk chocolate. I spent the remainder of that evening working him back outside, replacing the screen and luring him with a pan of milk around through five croquet wickets. These I pounded down while he was up to his greedy little tendrils in milk.

As Rover didn't free himself until midafternoon, I had a little free time to repair the line fence between our place and Abrell's. Pumpkin-vine spoor left no doubt that our Rover, for some reason, had flattened it.

In fact, for the next three mornings, I was required to resurrect the fence. On the third day, Gail Abrell dropped by. "You know," he said, leading up to the point of his mission, "I've seen it so dry that cows would give nothing but powdered milk. But for the past three days, my cows haven't produced so much as that." I hadn't experienced such a feeling in my stomach since the last time my wife told me she was pregnant. I laid low, offering him only a modicum of sympathy.

After he left, I went out and erected a 10-foot stockade fence between our place and his pasture field. For good measure, I strung an electric fence above that. And that night, I went to bed too tired to bother with the nonessentials, such as getting undressed. And a good thing it was, because no sooner had I fallen into a coma than my wife began drumming on my forehead with the evening paper and telling me "Gail is on the phone, and he sounds upset."

I managed to get in a sleepy "Yes?" before he launched into his soliloquy: "There's a pumpkin vine in our kitchen...pushed our back door right off the hinges...ran its dirty old stigma into a pitcher of milk on the table...milk that I had to buy—buy, mind you—because my cows aren't producing.., and I know why... that vine must have stripped them dry...and my wife has taken to bed...and there won't be any supper...and now the thing has just come out of the bathroom with a bottle of Milk of Magnesia..."

When he stopped to take a breath, I broke the connection and handed the hot receiver to my wife. "Call Lewis Service and tell them to send out a wrecker—the one with the winch Then come out to the garden. I'll get the saw."

While we were taking turns sawing Rover off at the base, the man with the winch drove up, and we began winching our wandering vine back home. Two hours later, Rover's insatiable stigma, wet from the pitcher of milk and still clutching the Magnesia bottle, hove into sight. Milk that had already drained from the lopped-off base had formed a small pond on Gail's side of the fence, enough to feed his pigs for a week. I hoped it would help set things straight. It might also help if I cut up Rover and gave him to Gail for ensilage. With this in mind, I began the formidable task of pulling the vine off the winch and stringing it to dry between the clothesline posts and the security light pole.

I was going pretty good, too, when I heard my wife yelling, "What in the world do you think you're doing?"

"Hmm...um...ah...getting Rover off the wrecker," I mumbled.

"You're pulling down the window curtains. What were you dreaming about anyway?"

"You aren't giving milk to any of those pumpkin vines!" I replied.

"What on earth brought *that* up!" she said, turning on the nightlight and hooking the curtain rod back in place.

"Never mind—just don't go near those vines with milk in any form. Even milk chocolate," I said.

"You are weird," she pointed out, turning off the light with a well-rehearsed, drawn-out sigh.

Chapter 12

WOMEN AND GASOLINE DON'T MIX

"You know that fan on the front of the engine?"

It was my wife calling from town. Two hours overdue and the highways having been given a "slick and hazardous" rating on the radio that morning—I had good reason to worry. During the first hour I took comfort in the thought that the car had slid off the road and she was keeping the wheels spinning until it ran out of gas. After the second hour I began praying, "Dear God, please bring Lois home safely—so I can kill her." Now, at last, she was on the phone.

"Yes, I know the fan in front of the engine. What about it?"

"My raincoat is twisted up in it, and the car won't start."

How does a woman manage to get her raincoat wrapped around that fan in front of the engine? Simple. She spreads her coat over the engine to protect it from moisture from the snow melting on the hood and forgets to remove it when she's through shopping and has finished grinding on the starter. And the fan grinds up the raincoat. It required a Shell service-station man and his assistant and $24 to get it unground.

The automobile, obviously, was not invented with the woman in mind. From the time Henry Ford put the horse out of business, the only concession the car people have made to the off sex is to go from basic black to a choice of colors. So instead of turning in our '72 Olds Cutlass the last time I moved up to a later vintage, I kept it for Lois to knock around in.

"A car of your very *own!*" was the way I phrased my sales pitch. "And I'm having Paul [the genius at Daniel's Garage who had several times saved the machine from the compactor) make a few alterations for your driving convenience."

I'll spare you the details. But among the conveniences were hard-rubber tires, a clear-plastic fuel tank visible above the windshield, and a full-length dresser drawer in place of that enigmatic instrument panel. I even stocked the drawer with her treasures from the old glove compartment:

Hair curlers, a 1963 Indianapolis city map, a handful of plastic spoons from McDonald's, a yellowed packet of Kleenex, four melted Life-Savers, three Wendy's ketchups, two Victoria Holt paperbacks, and a partridge in a pear tree (finger-painted three years ago by Kris, our grandson). This

Maynard Good Stoddard

still left room for Paul to install the windshield washer-wiper and the radio. Somehow he also managed to rig up an audio system that would announce emergencies such as "oil low" "...radiator boiling" "...muffler has fallen off." But not even Paul could foresee every contingency. "You know that thing that's supposed to spray the windshield?" She was calling again from town.

"Yes, what about it?" I asked, stretching the phone cord over to the sink, just in case.

"Only oil comes out," she said.

Yes, the woman I had taken for better or for worse—but certainly not for this—had filled the windshield washer with good old Kendall 10W40. Paul managed to get the container flushed, but the rubber hoses all had to be replaced.

Winter is an especially bad season for the woman on the road. Worse, of course, for the woman off the road—where one woman in particular spends hours at a time. We've already been kicked out of two motor clubs, and our membership in You Go or We Tow, Inc., is hanging by a thread.

In an attempt to be helpful without flaunting my God-given male superiority, I suggested she put a few bags of sand in the trunk to hold the rear end down and give the car better traction—especially coming up our driveway, which is more like a long ramp with a bend in the middle. If she got stuck she could put the sand under the wheels to keep them from spinning.

So what did she store in the trunk? Two 80-pound bags of "sand mix."

"I thought it was sand mixed with salt," she whimpered when I came home one night and found her car solidly cemented to our ramp about halfway up.

For the next two days I had to take a by-pass through the barnyard until I could find a man with a jackhammer to come and jackhammer the wheels loose. It may be summer before the last chunk of concrete breaks off the tires and her car no longer sounds like a two-tone grocery cart with a flat wheel.

In my naivete I had thought that winter could hold nothing more traumatic for a husband than getting an emergency call from his wife during a snowstorm. I had overlooked the theory widely held by women that the faster they can make the wheels churn, the faster the snow will melt down to solid footing, and the sooner they will be on their merry way. Given the time, sufficient fuel, and a car that wouldn't slide out of the ruts, this strategy might even work. But not in our driveway, with its 40-degree incline (or decline, depending on whether we are coming or going. And further depending on whether she knows the difference.)

Worse than an emergency phone call from your wife is to get nicely settled in robe and slippers on a wintry eve and have her come stomping in, shower wet snow on your magazine—and the dog asleep at your feet—and say, "You know that fence by the barnyard gate?"

"Yes, I know that fence. Why?"

"Well, it's sort of down. And the car is sort of on the other side."

Exchanging my robe for a mackinaw, my slippers for galoshes, and the comfort of the sofa in our snug living room for the frigid blast sweeping up our driveway, I floundered down to the feeble glow of the headlights and saw that the radiator was sending up steam signals of distress.

Not only did I find the fence sort of down, but the gate was also sort of horizontal. And three fence posts were definitely not perpendicular.

A cursory survey of the battlefield revealed that Lois had kept the wheels spinning faithfully until the back bumper had come to rest against a sassafras tree—at which point she had humbled herself to come up and ask for help.

Regardless of the number of years two people have continued to unite their plights in holy wedlock, or whatever, few opportunities are made-to-order like this for the male of the species to prove his superiority. Although my glasses were already frosted to zero visibility and snow from the sassafras packed the neck of my mackinaw as I shoveled out the wheels and spread sand in the tracks, I welcomed the challenge.

Finally, with everything "go" except for firing up the old bus and easing it out of there, I went back to the house and had Lois rewinterize herself and come down to watch. It was time she learned the proper technique for getting a car out of a seemingly hopeless...

"You should have signaled before I went sliding through Miller's fence," I said, as we floundered back to the house to call for a wrecker. "Flapped your arms or something. A man just naturally would have known that."

"I yelled for you to stop," she said. "I guess you couldn't hear me with the tires making so much noise. [Did I detect a note of sarcasm?], I thought maybe you were trying to show me how to go through a fence without leveling the posts. But you took out four to my three. Congratulations."

Just between us men, I'd forgotten about the lousy fence. And you know that driveway of Miller's? If I could only have kept the car sliding, I'd have hit it just right to be headed for the road.

But try explaining that to a woman—especially to one crass enough to count fence posts.

Chapter 13

OFF TO WORK SHE GOES

My wife had everything a woman could ask for. Besides me, there was a roof with only one leak over her head and access to a car that would usually start after pumping the accelerator a few times. She was also eating well, as our cowering bathroom scales will testify. So other than coming home with a $21.48 sack of groceries she could have carried in her teeth, why would any woman in her right mind (now *there's* a possibility) want to go back to work after all these years?

When we first united our plights in the trough of holy wedlock, or however that goes, she had been a practicing R.N. on private duty. Far be it from me to suggest that she used this noble calling as an excuse for dust in the refrigerator and meals that sometimes had to be thawed in the stomach. Let's just say I wasn't too upset when she knocked off "for a couple of weeks" to introduce our first child to this big old Wonderful World. Then somehow her hiatus stretched into 20-odd years and three-odd children. But now that they were all reared (one of the girls a little too much so), and she was suffering from an acute case of quilter's thumb, and was bringing home these $21.48 sacks of groceries she could carry in her teeth, she had somehow decided that it all added up to grounds for going back to work.

"If you do, so help me, I'll do the housework!" I threatened. She might have grimaced, but it's so hard to tell. "And the cooking!" No use. Even the thought of this embarrassment didn't faze her. When the woman gets an idea in her head (where an occasional one will lodge), it's as good as set in concrete. So I threw in the towel (which I should have saved to mop my forehead) and braced myself for a few start-up costs.

It's one thing to be braced—quite another to have your back against the wall. My little bride having gone from a scrawny size 12 to a healthy 16, the first outlay was for three uniforms at $24.95 per. In a futile effort to revive my spirits, she jokingly announced that her white shoes had been refused by Goodwill ten years ago. Luckily (her word, not mine), she found two pairs in her size on sale at a mere $19.88 the pair—plus lunch. Woman was not made to shop for shoes, I was told, on an empty stomach.

That evening I was pasting an "Out of Order" sign on the cover of our checkbook when the refurbished nurse led me into the living room to point out the spaghetti effect in the hand-braided rug. Turned out to be her former white stockings. Foolishly thinking that another acquisition would end the outgo before the income began coming in, I went along with the purchase of what had to be, even if she crawled to work on her hands and knees, a five-year supply of white panty hose.

How could I have overlooked the vital nurse' cap? And if you think a nurse can walk into a dollar store (nee dime store) and buy just any old white cap, you aren't any brighter than I am. A nurse, you see, must wear the cap of her alma mommie or run the risk of being drummed out of the Florence Nightingale corps or whatever.

Thus we shot an order off to the Henry Ford Hospital School of Nursing for three caps. And when she couldn't get the doggone things to stay on (I'm sorry, not only because I frown on the use of strong language but because it's an indication that one is losing the battle), she made a hair-styling appointment, valued (by the stylist) at $16.
"Why not a simple bob job for a couple of bucks?" I inquired. "With the cap in place, who would know?"
"I would know," she responded. And if you have an answer for that, please call me collect.
Not only was our checking account by now a disaster area eligible for a low-cost loan, but the cash I had cached for a surprise weekend fishing trip wouldn't have taken me to the nearest self-serve gas pump. The only reason I postponed filing for bankruptcy was the assumption that the nurse, finally, was ready to slap a Band-Aid on our wounded assets.

I have made better assumptions at race tracks. I had overlooked dues to the American Nurses' Association and the Indiana state registry. For another small fortune, a nursing bureau would phone at 4:30 a.m. to alert her to a case. Although alumnae dues were not all that much, they included a quarterly publication, the current issue of which reminded her of the Social Security obligations of the self-employed. Finally—or so I thought—just in case she'd forgotten which thermometer goes where, I took out a second mortgage on the house and bought malpractice insurance.
The question of transportation was answered quite simply—she would take the car. And how would I get around? Her answer was so clever: "As I see it, you have two choices:
Walk or jog."
The daily lunch money I 'lent' her would, as I understood it, be repaid with her first paycheck. The daily extras, I began to suspect, were being considered

out-and-out grants. I refer to such incidentals as the replacement for a hypodermic needle she broke while spearing olives out of a bottle the morning I couldn't come up with lunch money and she had to brown-bag it.. One day it was flowers for an aide who had taken the afternoon off after dropping a bedpan on her foot. Within a four-day stretch I underwrote two birthdays, a wedding, and chipped in to buy a Rolls-Royce for a retiring head nurse.

Payday, at last! Only a mother of twin daughters being wed in a double ceremony will appreciate my preparations for the big event. My dinner specialty—hot dogs, medium well—simmering on a back burner. Candles a-drip on the kitchen table. The dog sprayed with pine-scented room deodorizer. Lawrence Welk's "All of Me" at the ready on the record player. And all of little old apron-draped me smiling broadly in the doorway as my dear little thermometer caddy came aiming into the carport.

I assumed it was she, at any rate, it could as easily have been Raquel Welch with swollen legs. Legs were all that I could see when this figure finally emerged and began stumbling toward the door. The rest of the figure was hidden behind boxes, bundles, bales, bags... You name it, she had it.

In leading her up the steps I was able to name a few of the items. There was a pair of penguin door-stops we had been denying ourselves lo these many years. Here was a 2x3-foot framed print of "The End of the Trail" (if not essential, certain appropriate). Sticking out of one bag was the rubber fire hydrant our dog has been bugging us for since he was big enough to stand on three legs. Clamped in her teeth was the wire bail on a carton stamped "GOLDFISH."

"Is this all?" I asked, sarcastically, hoping she knew the meaning of the word.

"Eee erie uh iah urs ah oo doon." After I relieved her of the bail in her teeth, this became, "It's everything but my purse. And don't bother, there's nothing in it."

Among the essentials she proudly displayed that night was a ceramic cardinal that, when wound, trills "Oh What a Beautiful Morning." I have yet to wind it— nor will I, as long as our mornings begin at 4:30 a.m. and our checking account remains in intensive care.

I live for the day when she may begin to put her money some place besides the shopping malls. But I'm not banking on it.

Chapter 14

WHY WOMEN LIVE LONGER

The IRS has issued a new life-expectancy chart that for sanity is right up there with its 1040 form. In this rather important business of breathing in and out, it has both sexes ending in a dead heat. If one has made it to age 70, according to the chart, male and female alike are good for another 16 years. Survivors to age 75, be they named Harry or Harriett, still have another 12.5 years to dust off the old Bible and begin boning up for their finals.

I say rubbish! No, make that hogwash. I say the guy who prepared the chart has never been married a day in his life. Single people, yes, they might come out about even. But if the chartist had entered into his computer what the ravages of marriage do to hubby's life term, his figures would have given the female at least a dozen years more.

Don't tell me about equal stress in the marketplace now that the housewife has deserted the kitchen cabinet for the filing cabinet. I'm saying hogwash because of the ravages that take their toll when the housewife isn't filing.

"Do you want to go out, Brutus?" the longer-liver will ask our dog, who is standing with his front paws on the doorknob, back legs crossed, tongue out, tears in his eyes. Not once in ten years has Brutus replied, "Yeah, I'd kinda like to go out, if it's not too much trouble."

Of course it's not too much trouble. Because this question is my cue to heave myself off the sofa, whack my knee on the corner of our glass-topped coffee table (I don't think I've missed once since she bought the stupid thing), and let the dog out.

"I can't remember turning off the stove," Lois will muse after climbing into the car and fastening her seat belt. Interpreted, this means, "Why don't you shove the thingamajig into Park, shut off the engine, unbuckle, and go in to check?"

Let the telephone ring (especially after we're in bed) and she will say, "Is that for you?" You know, as many times as I've heard that telephone, I still can't tell a male ring from a female ring. On these occasions it is my custom to whack both knees on the coffee table. The fact that it's usually a female ring doesn't help a whole lot.

The responsibility for keeping the movable parts of our household and yardhold appliances moving falls upon you-know-who. If a part is burnoutable, why be concerned if it burns out?—the replacement also falls on hubby's side of the work ledger. And should the job be beyond his limited talents, it's up to him to call in one of those chaps in the white-denim jumpers at 20 bucks an hour, plus parts, plus service charge.

As a result, rather than making our water pump start up, I shave with water Lois has used for boiling eggs. She, on the other hand, thinks nothing of activating the pump by letting the water run until it's hot enough to wet her bangs. (Who ever heard of wetting bangs with cold water?) I try to make up for the wear and tear on the hot-water heater by taking my summer baths down at the creek and beating myself against a rock.

She'll put the vacuum sweeper in action to suck up nothing more than a wisp of navel lint from the bedroom floor. I pick up flakes of artificial snow from under the Christmas tree by hand. She heats the car in winter and air-conditions it in summer just to drive to the mailbox at the foot of our driveway. In rain or snow or dark of night, I walk to the mailbox. She turns up the thermostat to dry the panty hose she won't be wearing for another week. To spare the furnace, I dry my socks on my feet.

Consider the refrigerator. A man pretty well knows what he's after before opening the door. If I'm putting in rather than taking out, I can yank the door open and stick the stuff in before the motor realizes I'm there. My best time for a bowl of Jell-O, a dish of coleslaw, and a carton of eggs is seven seconds. Oh, a little coleslaw might plop into the Jell-O, but the eggs have to be cracked sometime anyway, as I point out at the inquisition.

Women, on the other hand, are browsers. My wife especially delights in opening the door and just standing there, humming. Maybe she'll finally stick a finger tentatively into a bowl and mutter, "That looks like coleslaw in the Jell-O." Or she'll lift a cover from a casserole and muse, "That must be the Hungarian goulash from last Thursday...I'd better fry it tomorrow for breakfast."

Not until the fridge has begun to vibrate nicely will she begin to move things. Sometimes she moves things from one shelf to another; sometimes she moves things to a new location on the same shelf. Sometimes she indulges in a game of "refrigerator checkers" by jumping one dish over another and sticking the jumped dish out on the table. Then she'll begin putting everything she can into smaller receptacles. By this time the furnace has come on, and she is standing there with frosted eyebrows and wondering what it was she wanted in the first place.

Counterclockwise, the electric range has no movable parts. So anyone from an alien planet might think it's beyond a woman's touch. It has, however, an $80 thermostat that can fall victim to overuse. Ergo, while I am sparing the toaster by eating stale rye bread and pretending it is toast, wife is charring her bread in the oven. While I'm wearing a sweater on chilly mornings, she not only starts up the furnace but turns all four range burners on High, turns the oven to Bake, and leaves the oven door open. By the time we sit down to a breakfast of cold cereal,

NOTHING SERIOUS, I HOPE

the mercury on the thermometer outside the kitchen window is trying to get out at the top.

One of the more subtle ways a wife has of cutting down on hubby's life span is in the moving of furniture. Coming home late one night from an exhausting game of golf that went to the 19th hole, I considerately removed my shoes before tippy-toeing upstairs. And so as not to awaken sleeping beauty, I undressed in the dark and hung my clothes on the floor before going over and dropping exhausted onto the bed. Only it wasn't the bed. From the tinkling of vials and the crash of bottles and jars I surmised I had landed on the vanity. For the next three days I carried the aura of an Avon lady stuck in a revolving door in mid-August.

Then there are the instructions a wife leaves with hubby when she's to be away for a three-day flower-arrangement seminar, or whatever. The Lima-beans episode must have shortened my time on earth by a full six weeks.

"All you have to do," she said, "is wash them, let them soak awhile, put them in a pan, be sure there's water in the pan, and put the pan on the burner. And oh yes, turn the burner on. Do you know how?"

Of course I know how to turn the burner on. But how do you wash a Lima bean? When I couldn't find where she hides the vegetable brush, I made my toothbrush do. Holding on to those little devils while dipping the brush in a dish of Dove is not the easiest trick in my repertoire. By the time I did 25 (salvaging 23; 2 got away from me and shot underneath the stove), I decided I had enough for a mess.

Soak them awhile, she said. Without a chart showing the number of minutes in awhile, I gave them a full ten minutes before putting them on the stove and turning on the burner. After the water came to a boil, I gave them another ten minutes and then spooned one out to test it. This maneuver left me with 22—the thing skidded out from under my testing fork and joined the 2 underneath the stove.

Fifteen minutes later, afraid the beans would turn to mush, I ladled them onto a plate. Right away I knew my fears were groundless—mushy beans don't rattle. Still, I had to prove it by chipping the enamel on my best tooth before dumping the beans into my tackle box. If I can figure a way to drill holes in their little carcasses, they'll make ideal sinkers.

When the routine gets a little dull at our house, woman enjoys no greater thrill than making a dramatic phone call to hubby at the office. "Your refrigerator is shot!" is high on the list, closely followed by "Your furnace just blew up!" An appliance is "ours" only when new and being shown off to envious neighbors. Once the thing is shot or blows up, it's all yours, buddy. I've had calls on everything from "The wires on your space heater have melted!" to "Your electric carving knife is stuck in the curtain rod I was trying to shorten!" to "I got only three walnuts cracked, and now your ice-cube crusher just sits there and whines!"

When it comes to knocking years off a man's life span, a wife counts heavily upon the car—like the time my wife drove to Spencer to buy a new belt for her sewing machine, the old belt having given up the ghost midway through sewing up a stuffed turkey.

"Your car won't run!" she yelled into the phone, without even the courtesy of the customary preface "Guess what?"

The car, it seems, had died on her third pass at parallel parking in front of Hanlon Brothers Hardware. My own automotive skills being limited to kicking the tires and reading the dipstick, I suggested she might better have spent her quarter calling the service department at Algood Chevrolet. Her cool "Thanks a lot" and the clicking of the phone left no doubt what the main topic of conversation would be when she came home.

Sure enough. Algood's had diagnosed her trouble as being out of gas. And why in the world hadn't I checked the tank before she left? And in the heat of her monologue her bangs dried out. So they had to be watered. This started the pump. And the wet bangs brought on a chill. Which meant turning on the range and opening the oven door. Which caused the refrigerator to begin refrigerating. Which caused me to head for the creek. You guessed it. Not another bath, just another beating myself against the rock.

Chapter 15

STRESS: MARRIAGE VS. JAIL TERM

I have just come across a chart listing "Life's Events According to Stress." And the reason I am taking typewriter in hand (no mean trick in itself) is to complain about "Marriage" being placed way down in the No. 7 spot. That isn't the worst of it. What has really got my hackles up is that "Jail Term" has been rated No. 4, for Pete's sake!

There are husbands, I'm sure, who would go so far as to say that the two entries are synonymous. But not me, brother. I may be in enough trouble for suggesting that the questionnaire that gathered the information must have been sent to wives and bachelors only.

When it comes to the event called Marriage, I have been a participant since December 7, 1941. (Or was that the beginning of our war with Japan? I get the two dates confused.) Anyway, when it comes to stress, I have come to envy the wet bird perched on a high-tension wire and scratching out lice.

A wet bird has never had to lather its face with Cool Whip because the last of its shaving cream was used in decorating the Christmas tree.

A wet bird has never known the stress of hearing its mate call through the bathroom door, "I forgot to tell you, I painted the toilet seat!"

A wet bird has never been required to return a pound cake to the Kroger store because it weighed only 14 1/2 ounces.

A wet bird has never answered the phone to hear his mate say, "Hanlon Bros. Hardware doesn't have a two-inch socket wrench. Should I get two one-inchers?"

Much of the stress in marriage, according to other authorities, arises from money. Not money per se but the lack thereof. Of which we have plenty. Of lack, that is. The way my mate gets rid of money you'd think that it was printed by lepers. And that the quicker she can get rid of the stuff, the less risk she runs of having her skin fall off.

Sales are one of the favorite conveniences for saving her hide. If this woman who united her plight with mine in the trough of holy wedlock, or however that goes, sees a $12.95 lobster pot reduced to $7.98, I might as well begin taking off the car door and removing the back seat, because she's going to buy it. It matters not that the nearest lobster is 900 miles from Owen County, Indiana, as long as she beat the lobster-pot retailers out of a handsome $4.97.

Another stress that has raised its ugly head at our house concerns hubby's staying home while wife, an R.N., is employed. Made all the more stressful when wife is convinced that free-lance writing and retirement are one and the same. I am equally convinced that a wife keeps a score sheet on her husband's peccadilloes when she is in charge of the housework. We're talking here of maybe leaving the cap off the toothpaste tube, hanging his pajamas on the bedroom floor, polishing his black shoes on her white cat—little things like that. Now along comes the old switcheroo: she's out of the house and he's at home. And he's going to pay...pay...PAY!

In those halcyon days when I would come home from selling pantyhose door-to-door, my dear wife would have the house so tidy I'd think company was coming. Today, she isn't home ten minutes before our joint could qualify for a federal loan as a disaster area.

The bathroom in particular is where she becomes a horse of a different color, you might say. *(You* might say it, but not me, brother.) The things that come out of her hair alone are enough to camouflage the lavatory top and the toilet-tank cover.

The other night I saw something wiggling in the mess and killed it with my shaving cream can. After its demise wife let me know that I had demised her one and only "switch." And she wouldn't even help me clean the shaving cream off the walls and the ceiling.

There's another little matter. Now that I am preparing the meals (or mess, as she jokingly refers to them) and she has the latest thing in dishwashers—a husband at home—wife thinks nothing of emptying the cupboards at every meal. Frankly, I don't think much of it myself.

Take breakfast alone. It's separate spoons for coffee, grapefruit, and oatmeal, a knife for scraping the toast, another for spreading the butter. What she does with a fork is beyond me, unless she uses it to scratch her head. And I never have enough dishes on the table. Don't be surprised if the next issue of the *Guinness Book of World Records* lists me as the only man to wear out a set of dishes by washing.

In the meantime, I am bending over backward trying to hold dirty dishes to a minimum. If I use the meat cleaver for hacking up a butternut squash, I use the cleaver for paring the potatoes and dicing the carrots. I'll admit it's not easy spreading margarine on whole-wheat bread with a meat cleaver, but it can be done. I've found it is also possible to eat your salad off a Job Squad paper towel.

Eating ice cream from the scoop, however, I can't recommend. After I got my tongue caught under that little metal ejector a few nights ago, I was obliged to call upon you-know-who to extricate me.

Another marriage stress that by no means helps the blood-pressure reading concerns her shopping for groceries on her way home from work. Her morning ritual is to crumble the last of the bread in the house for the birds, leaving me to construct my luncheon sandwich out of left-over butternut squash laminated between two soda crackers. Which is also for the birds, if she wants my

NOTHING SERIOUS, I HOPE

opinion—which she hasn't asked for yet. The highlight of my midday dining of late has been a slab of cheese too hard for the mousetraps and a doggie bag from Ponderosa that wife forgot to feed to the dogs. And then she comes waddling in at night with a head of lettuce and a can of crushed pineapple for our dinner. Seems she is still stuffed from her cafeteria luncheon menu of beef and noodles, baked potato, creamed corn, and hot rolls, with Bavarian cream pie to fill in the chinks.

The third half of stress in our marriage (two halves can't cover it all) has to do with her laundry and the few little items I add from time to time. "Would you like to knock off washing windows and go to town with me?" was her subtle approach one Saturday morning. "I've got some laundry to do."

Since I was done with the windows anyway, except for the one in the shed and those in either end of the attic, I like an innocent lamb to the slaughter, let her untie the hard knot with which she had secured my rubber apron, and we drove to Spencer. There, after graciously toting her basket of clothes into the Old Sock laundry, I sat down with a copy of the *Evening World* that had evidently managed somehow to survive the rinse cycle.

"Watch me now," my mate called before I'd even had time to interpret the headline. So I watched her blithely toss the clothes into the washer, gaily fling in a handful of detergent, and complacently deposit three quarters into the slot. "There, do you think you can handle that?" she triumphantly asked.

The opinion you may have already formulated of me to the contrary, I'm no dummy. Of course I could handle that. A kid could handle that. But I haven't been able to hire one to do it.

Now that I have got my feet wet (an understatement), I have found that the laundry is the social center of Spencer. More to the point, the clientele runs 98 percent to healthy young women. And they get in each other's way trying to teach me the fine points of laundering.

My next-of-tub approached me one day, wiping her face on a pillow slip, and explained that it wasn't necessary to lift the lid on my machine to peek in and see how things were going. And there was the time I left my glasses at home, hoping to look virile rather than studious, and a lovely specimen of womanhood took the trouble to inform me that I was putting oatmeal instead of detergent into my machine. It was the longest day I've ever spent.

As for Jail Term being rated three notches ahead of Marriage on that stress chart, the wives and bachelors should have been around when I surprised my dear wife one night by having her pantyhose all ironed when she came home. That would have scrambled their ratings for good. And I haven't even mentioned a wife's way with things mechanical. Nor am I about to. Our marriage has enough stress as it is.

Chapter 16

TO SLEEP, PERCHANCE—

Do you know why a baby can sleep 22 hours out of 24? Because a baby (we're talking male baby here) isn't married, that's why. Let one of those little suckers tie the knot, and if he closes his eyes for 2 hours out of the 24 he's lucky.

When I was single, I could go to sleep on a picket fence. No problem. I did even better in my two o'clock Spanish class in college. But after uniting my plight with a member of the opposing sex through the ritual of holy wedlock, take it from me, *moy buenos amigos,* or *muy buen amigi,* or is it *me hon ami?*—I haven't enjoyed what you'd call the sleep of the drugged since.

My wife, who has a Ph.D. in husband waking, has made waking me up her life's work. One of her favorite strategies is to turn off the TV while I'm lying on the sofa and watching a ball game. One time it was to get me to taste some questionable leftover stew before she fed it to her precious cat, Snowflake (or Flaky, as I choose to call her). Running a close second to the delight of waking me up is the satisfaction my wife derives from preventing my going to sleep in the first place.

The Cockroach Caper was one of her most successful machinations. While dallying in the express lane at the supermarket, she had read the front page of one of those weird weeklies, which claimed you could get rid of roaches by sprinkling baking soda in their runways. Seems the little fellers eat the soda, and being unable to burp, they have no alternative but to blow up. And by golly, it worked. I spent the next three nights lying wide-eyed in bed while I listened to cockroaches explode. There goes one now.

Or take the time I was going to drink a glass of warm milk before retiring. While the milk was heating in the pan, my dear wife, thinking I was preparing my favorite dish—eggs in milk over toast—slipped in an egg for herself. I thought the milk poured into the glass rather lumpily, but because the only light came from the refrigerator, I gave the matter no further thought—until the egg came sliding down, that is, and slapped me in the face. And by the time I had chased the thing out of my pajamas, my adrenaline was at high tide for the night.

I've counted enough sheep to give every tick in Australia a flock of its own. But this stratagem is so boring I always begin fooling around. When the sheep are in midair, I'll raise the fence. Or I'll hang a wire from their necks and make them hurdle an electric fence. (You never saw such jumping.)

I once tried taking sleeping pills—or thought I did. My dear wife, who didn't think they were good for me, substituted saltpeter. "Killed two birds with one stone," she later explained during intermittent shrieks of laughter.

My dear wife can read herself to sleep in minutes. Considering the stuff she reads in those paperbacks, it's easy to understand. But let her prop *Gibbon's Decline and Fall of the Roman Empire* or the *Encyclopaedia Britannica* on her chest, as I do, and she couldn't so much as toss and turn, much less go to sleep.

Last night—or was it the night before? or last week? (it's hard to reckon time when you don't sleep)—I gave Morpheus a full half hour before finally giving up and turning on the night light.

"Where have you been?" my dear wife grunted.

"I haven't *been,*" I replied. "I'm trying to go—to sleep.

"Have you tried turning out the light and closing your eyes?" she suggested, rolling over and pulling the sheet over her head. At the moment, it improved her looks considerably.

Not wanting to rouse my sleep buds further by hoisting *Decline and Fall* on my chest, I picked up her paperback.

Turned out to be the classic *Case of the Coughing Corpse*. "A book you can't put down," boasted the blurb on the front.

And it wasn't far wrong, for someone had spilled honey on the cover. And you talk about mystery—it was a mystery from the word go. The first four pages were missing.

However, like a snail with a charley horse, sleep finally began creeping up on me. Laying the book quietly on the night stand, I reached over, turned out the light, and then ever so gently pulled up the covers and closed my eyes.

"Bet you don't know who did it!" came this clacking at my side. And it was good night, John, I've brought your saddle home, as the saying goes.

"The butler."

"Way off."

"I really don't care."

"You'd never guess anyway."

By getting up four times to splash cold water on my face, I finished the book just before daybreak. Turned out the victim had done himself in from a habit calling for four packs of cigarettes a day. Not only did he cough himself to death—strange sounds could be heard coming from the grave for the next three days. A free epitaph chiseled in marble had been offered by the tobacco people:

It wasn't the cough
That carried him off:
It was the coffin
They carried him off in.

Into the life of every married man there come times when, through some fluke, he gets a night out on his own.

NOTHING SERIOUS, I HOPE

His wife may be spending the evening with her mother, discussing new ways of keeping hubby awake. So hubby drags in at 5:45 a.m., too tired to take off his shoes before hitting the old sack. And who is the bright-eyed reception committee of one awaiting him in bed? It's not Flaky the cat.

Oh, the unbridled joy of the maltreated wife on such occasions. Nothing else in the inventory of female emotions can approach it. Since the crime is most often committed on a Saturday night, the poor culprit will be home on Sunday, when the slightest evidence of weariness can be detected.

I well recall my own abused wife's inspirations upon several of these glorious opportunities:

"Let's move it, chum. Anyone who can stay out all night certainly has the constitution to mow the lawn without lying down between laps."

"Of course we're going for a Sunday drive! If you can keep your eyes open for 29 hours straight, they should be used to it by now."

"That's right, stay out all night and then be grumpy just because the kids dump you out of the hammock!"

"You know very well we're going to the movies tonight. Now come down off that picket fence and get your jacket on."

Researching the insomnia experts hasn't helped. One idiot suggested that listening to a repetitious sound would do the trick. I had my doubts right from the start. I've been listening to a repetitious sound now for more than I care to remember, but one night in desperation I thought I'd give it a shot. Stumbling out of bed and fumbling my way into the bathroom, I sat on the edge of the tub and turned on the cold water tap to a steady glib...glob...glup...glib...glob...glup, etc. The next thing I knew, my dear wife was slapping me back to life and leading me to the bed. The next thing after that, she was telling me for heaven's sake to get out of the bed with those wet pajamas.

My heart by this time beating in something more than three-quarter time, I would listen to it. By lying face down I could make the old ticker tick 'em off loud and clear. Thump...thump...thumpity thump...thump...thump. thumpity thump...thump..._____ thump. What, what, what! I sat up. Was my imagination playing tricks, or was I a thumpity short? By this time the cadence of the old pump was banking off the walls: thump...thump _____ thump. No doubt about it, I was hitting on only three cylinders. I pulled up the sheet to wipe the sweat off my brow.

"What on earth are you doing now?" dear wife groaned.

"It's my heart," I groaned back.

"Well stop it."

"But it's missing."

"We'll look for it in the morning," she mumbled, turning over and jabbing her toenails into my leg.

Maynard Good Stoddard

No need to worry her, I thought bravely. I just won't listen to that thump...thump_____sssooosh! Oh no! My main dike must have given way.

"Get a doctor!" I gasped. "I'm going—"
"Don't...forget...rubbers," she muttered.

I spent the rest of the night on the sofa. It would be much easier for the men in the white coats to carry me out in the morning.

"To sleep: perchance to dream: ay, there's the rub;/For in that sleep of death what dreams may come/When we have shuffled off this mortal coil,/Must give us pause." So wrote Mr. William Shakespeare in another tragic work under the title of *Hamlet*.

From the way it looks, except for twin beds, or twin bedrooms, or changing mattresses, or changing wives, shuffling off this mortal coil is about my only hope for getting more than two hours of sleep a night. Whatever the dreams that may come, they'll be more than welcome.

Chapter 17

MY LIFE IN A GREENHOUSE

My dear wife was making an emergency run into town. Either to get an earring welded or buy sleeping pills for the cat, I've forgotten which.

"As long as you're going," I called from beneath the sink where I was disengaging the trap to look for a fugitive false eyelash, "would you mind buying me a football helmet so I won't keep knocking myself silly on those blasted hanging plants of yours?"

Two hours later she returned, all aflutter—which was not altogether out of character—having forgotten the cat's sleeping pills, or whatever, and the football headgear, but, joy of joys, she *had* timed her trip to coincide with the biggest plant sale in the history of K mart. Car trunk full, back seat fuller, African violets sitting on the instrument panel, weeping willows strapped to the roof.

What else had she added to her current foliage menagerie? She had no idea. They had sort—of Latin names, she thought. As I brought up the wheelbarrow to help her unload, I wept copiously, directing my tears toward several specimens that looked as if they'd appreciate the moisture, remembering the dozen foot-high "Mountain Olives, or Harvest Olives, or something like that," that she had brought home to make a hedge along the drive. That hedge is already 20 feet high, obliging us to drive behind the grape arbor and across the garden to reach the road. The parsnips are getting pretty tired of it.

I hold the state of Indiana responsible for some of my problems—for offering trees in 200-unit lots at bargain prices. And if you know women and bargain prices, you'll believe that my big blue eyes were opened one morning by a UPS delivery horn, announcing the arrival of three lots, or 600 trees. And if you've ever planted 600 trees in clay soil, you'll also believe that my once-regal stature ended up reminiscent of a croquet wicket. It hasn't improved a whole lot since.

It is not so much her outdoor flora that has turned me into a contemporary Dr. LivingStone, however. Except for the hedge, we (flora and I) enjoy a fairly good rapport. The four redbuds that cost the price of a new set of golf clubs, including bag, have yet to sprout a twig. Anything that *has* managed to come alive on our billiard-ball clay knoll I can walk around or jump over. Or, if the situation permits, step squarely upon. And, due to some careless mowing on my part, I no longer have to fight my way down to the mailbox. Not that I didn't hear about it. In fact, a boiler factory hath no noise like that of a woman whose wisteria hath been shorn at the roots.

"You should have fenced it," I suggested during the inquisition.

"Anyone who can't tell wisteria—if that's what it was—from simple grass shouldn't be operating a mower," rebutted Mrs. Luther Burbank several times removed. I noticed the other day that the stuff is coming back again, which may bring on another case of ignorance in a couple of weeks.

Although the problems of an outdoor jungle are sufficient for any man, they are as nothing compared to the jungle this man has to contend with within the confines of his own castle, as a bachelor poet once referred to it.

Having beaten me to retirement, my dear wife has embraced with unparalleled bliss the lethal hobby known as macrame. This is the fiendish pastime of suspending plants in cast-iron buckets from the ceiling. Her greatest enjoyment comes from hanging them at a level carefully gauged to catch a man of six feet just above the eyebrows. A woman of 5'5" or less can, of course, sail under with no thought of a contusion or a concussion or having her head molded into the contour of a Hubbard squash. And once the husband has spoiled the game by remembering where the booby traps have been placed and begins walking along the back of the sofa to get from kitchen to bedroom, the wife accepts the challenge and redistributes the buckets, and the contest begins all over again.

For a little diversion during dinner a few nights ago, the wife I know best (which isn't saying much) rigged up a dandy. Slumping into my chair at the table, not fully recovered from a beaut she had nailed me with just inside the kitchen door, I was just beginning my salad, which looked to be a clever combination of daisy stems and moss roses, when I felt something crawling on the back of my neck. With visions of black widow spiders dancing in my head, I didn't want to lay down my fork before reaching back to deliver a terminal wallop to whatever it was. What I succeeded in doing was burying all five tines of my fork in my left ear lobe. And not until my dear wife had laughingly plugged my wound with a paper towel did I learn that I had been attacked by nothing more perilous than a trailing arbutus she had suspended only that day behind my place at the table.

It naturally followed that my nightmare that night consisted of having the thing trail us into town, forcing me to step out of line at the box office and send it home: "You go home! Go on now, git! No, you can't see the movie!" And everybody was hissing and booing me as the vine finally turned around, put its little stigma between its calyxes, or whatever, and slunk away.

Our closed-in front porch I had conceived as a lovely bit of desert in our lush six-room oasis. A place where we could sit on long summer evenings without having any mosquitoes drain our blood or moths chew up our clothes. My dear wife offered not the slightest hint that the 12 windows would make the area ideal for a combination greenhouse-nursery and a proving ground for unidentifiable aberrations of nature. Not word one to indicate that the foot-wide board she requested beneath the windows would immediately disappear beneath a battery of pots, crocks, jars, bottles, a discarded hand basin, and four feet of leftover gutter, all sprouting flora designed either to run down the wall and across the floor to make walking a hazard, or to spread across the windows to obscure the view, our sole reason for buying this hilltop clayheap in Freedom, Indiana, in the first place.

One day, upon noticing that I could still wedge in a coffee cup on the extreme end of the board, she immediately plugged the gap with a bunch of cups containing cherry-tomato seedlings.

"Well, at last you've done something that makes a little sense," I said. "But why all this other crud when most of it could just as well be laid to rest in your so-called rock garden? Or would that disturb your weed arrangement out there?"

"I have the plants inside because they take in carbon dioxide and give off oxygen," she sniffled.

"I'll buy you a respirator," I offered. "You've got so much junk in this jungle if one of us ever has hay fever he'll be dead before he can get to the couch."

"You wait until these are all in bloom," she said, tenderly pulling a wayward vine off the ceiling and draping it over the last hope of visibility through the eight front windows, "you'll be eating your remarks." I could have retorted they would be an improvement over her daisy-stem and moss-rose salad, but I thought better of it.

I moved the cherry tomatoes out to the garden just in time. They're already five feet tall, and counting. Too bad we didn't have them for a hedge instead of those Mountain Olives, or whatever they are. As for the front porch, my dear wife still fights her way out there with a watering can whenever she isn't hanging up a new bell ringer.

As for me, I have written the porch off altogether. The closest I approach it now is the doors that give out onto it. And only then whenever one of her eager-beaver vines has come creeping in over the threshold. That's where I put my foot down. If my dear wife isn't looking, that is.

Chapter 18

TRY NOT TO BLEED

I have bled in all 50 states except Alaska and Colorado. The reason for these omissions: I've never been to Alaska, and my dear wife didn't accompany me to Colorado. She *was* with me in Mexico, Canada, France, England, Holland, Belgium, West Germany, Switzerland, and Austria, and I have bled in those countries, too. I missed out on little Liechtenstein only because we passed through before she could come up with an excuse for opening one of my main arteries. As for Hawaii, she says she had nothing to do with my falling over the trash container after gawking at the girls in dental-floss bikinis. I say she could have hollered "Trash Container!" or "Look out!" or something.

Her main weapon on these foreign junkets is her suitcase. She delights in leaving it on the main route to the bathroom. Then when I'm stumbling toward the door at night I at least fall over it. If this should send me charging headlong into the wall, so much the better.

Her greatest triumph occurred in Vienna the night I plunged out an open patio door. I was spared the embarrassment of going over the balcony rail only by colliding with a wrought-iron chair. As luck would have it, I crawled back to bed suffering nothing more serious than what is listed in the lexicon of football injuries as a hip pointer.

Because my wife has packed everything imaginable into her suitcase, she has to call on me to close the thing. This is usually good for a dislocated knee from trying to bring the two sides together. And if I fail to get my best finger half severed by one of the snaps, she gives me a second chance on the handle she pulls the thing with. Still, that's better than risking a hernia by having to carry her bag as well as my own, besides her coat, my coat, her overnight case, two umbrellas, a packet of travel folders, and a sack of souvenirs. *She* has her purse to lug all over the place, you know. I have scraped my shins to the bone trying to help her into a bobbing Hovercraft for the trip from Cancun to Cozumel. I have had my left shoulder all but paralyzed from being leaned on while mounting the steps of the pyramid at Chichen Itzâ. I've had press-on nails pressed a full inch into my back during a tram ride up the Stanserhorn mountain in the Swiss Alps. But for all the satisfaction my dear wife gets from seeing my blood flow in foreign countries, it's home-sweet-and-sour-home where she hits her stride.

NOTHING SERIOUS, I HOPE

The Furniture Caper is one of her favorites. She began this assault by stocking our living room with two end tables and a coffee table having matching glass tops. Sure, someone with 20/20 vision can see the corners of those things. But for someone who has trouble just finding the doorway to this torture chamber, they are murder—or as close to it as I care to come.

Have you ever seen a girded tree, whose bark has been peeled off in a strip around the trunk so it will die of its own accord? Then you know how my legs look after 11 years of hitting the corners of the coffee table with my shins, my calves, and the tenderized flesh in between. The few times I've remembered to detour coincide with the times I hit my shin on the end table. And the funny thing is, says my dear wife, that's when I jump back and gash the calf of my leg on the coffee table—which sends me forward again. In other words, it's just one grand circus.

Changing the location of the furniture has also proved effective. In a man's garage, the car goes here, the mower is there, the stepladder over there and so on. He can find what he wants blindfolded. But the distaff side can't leave the television in one corner of the room for longer than a week without switching it with the easy chair. Not that I have ever tried to tune in Wheel of Fortune" on the easy chair, but I did give my tail bone a week's sabbatical by dropping onto the television one night before turning on the floor lamp.

Then there are the foreign objects she loves to plant in my normal route to the aforementioned floor lamp. The cleverest of these, to date, are the quilting frames. Had they been erected I might have escaped with nothing more serious than a fractured pelvis. As it was, they tripped me up, sending me headfirst into the wall and then bottom first onto the floor register. Luckily, I don't belong to a nudist colony, because for the next three days my right flank could have been mistaken for a waffle.

Concerned that I might have damaged the frames, borrowed only that afternoon from Alma Walters, my dear wife hopped over me to turn on the light. Finding the frames O.K., she asked, as an afterthought, "Are you hurt?"

Why, no. How could a man get hurt by ramming his head into a wall and falling backward onto the floor register?

I still carry scars on my once-noble brow from the den affair. My dear wife, not having made me bleed for three days straight and evidently thinking this might be bad for my circulatory system (I have no overflow tank), volunteered to help me install bookshelves in this room where I put words to paper. Nor could I talk her out of it.

The supports for the shelves are the kind that have a metal track running up the wall. Brackets fit the slots in the track, and then the bracket hooks are tapped down. My dear, dear wife, in her enthusiasm to get the job done, failed to tap down the brackets for the top shelf. So I was handing the last of the books up to her when—what to my surprise—I was greeted by a cascade of shelf, books, and brackets that brought me to my knees and my head to rest on a marble-top table.

"If you are going to use language like that," she said, after I had regained my faculty of speech, "I'm not going to help you anymore." It was my first break since she came down with lockjaw.

Of the many strategies the dear woman employs for keeping my blood level below the dipstick requirement, she relies most heavily upon the stepstool. It has beaten out even those cast-iron pots she hangs from the ceiling, with which she is reshaping my head into the contour of a Hubbard squash.

Nor am I forgetting the miniature ponies she supposedly took on as a hobby. They actually were for the sole purpose of getting me up at 2 a.m., so I could retrieve them from the neighbors' while they took turns chewing on the calves of my legs and knocking me into the ditch. I'm still looking for a pair for glasses out there in the bushes somewhere.

One of her favorite stunts with the stepstool was to have me mount the top step to jump on a board she wanted broken. She had prepared the board by supporting each end on a cement block. The board being rotten on the underside, I went right through it, sprained both ankles, and had a fairly satisfactory hole opened in my right earlobe by one end of the board.

I had no more than nicely healed from this duplicity than—under the pretext of running a wire from a corner of the house to the elm tree for the dog to run on—she invited me up on the stepstool again. What she really had in mind, once I was up there holding one end of the wire, was to pull on the other end ("to make it nice and straight," you know) before I had my end secured to the house. By so doing, of course, she succeeded in pulling me off the stool and onto the brick walk leading to the shed. The stains are still there.

There are times the stepstool is not quite high enough and the stepladder too high for what the dear woman has in mind, and she has to come up with something in between—like the contrivance she came up with this past Christmas season.

I had come slogging into the house after an unscheduled hour of aerobics from trying to catch up with a snow blower that took advantage of my gift for falling down by blowing stones instead of snow the length of our two-track driveway and back. And this clever woman had obviously timed the placing of the angel atop our Christmas tree to coincide with my entrance. For this purpose she had erected a scaffold consisting of an end table, the ottoman, and two volumes of the Encyclopaedia Britannica. And she was making a pretense of scaling this precarious construction when, in my stupor, I said, "Here, I'll do that. You'll fall and break your neck."

So saying, I mounted the makeshift setup, stretched up to anchor the angel on the spike at the top of the tree—and came to on the floor behind the sofa. "If you're going to bleed," my dear wife was saying, checking the angel for damage, "please do it over the poinsettia. I just cleaned the carpet."

With great will power, I didn't bleed a drop. I wouldn't give her the satisfaction.

Maynard Good Stoddard

Chapter 19

A KINDER, GENTLER MARRIAGE

How do you know when the honeymoon is over? You get a pretty good idea the morning your dear wife asks, "Before putting your shoes on, would you mind walking around right here?—I can't find the thumbtack I just dropped."

Our romantic relationship was not strengthened a whole lot when later that morning as I removed my one coat from the closet, the wooden pole slipped its moorings and all 18 of her coats landed in a heap on the floor. As I set a new record for closing the outside door behind me, I was left to speculate whether her parting remark had to do with my fixing the rod or something about God.

In either case, instead of stopping at Melick's on the way home for a dozen long-stemmed roses, I saved $32 by stopping at the Spencer-Owen Public Library for this book dealing with how to keep romance alive after marriage. Although the author was a movie star with only two husbands to her credit, I figured she might still have picked up a few pointers in the romance department that my dear wife and I had overlooked.

The recurring theme of the book—not finding a new lover but making a new lover out of old hubby—I can't argue with. What I do argue with is that the approach might well be feasible with the Hollywood crowd, but for the bunch in Freedom, Indiana, I'm afraid these tactics aren't worth a snowball in you-know-where.

"Wake your husband at daybreak to hear the birds sing" is one snappy sentiment. To which I reply: If my wife ever wakes me at daybreak to hear the birds sing, she'll be hearing the birds sing for the next two days. Currently she wakes me at daybreak only to tell me that the furnace hasn't come on. And that is often enough.

I did try out the next idea: "Don't eat the same food in the same way; take off for other places...keep an element of unpredictability between you." I took off for Spencer and told my dear wife we would be dining at McDonald's—then surprised her by going to Hardee's. Another time I actually went to McDonald's—but to the drive-in window, and we ate in the car. However, it didn't seem to do much for our romance. Next time I may light a candle on the instrument panel.

Another jim-dandy suggestion for keeping the old romancebuds alive involves serving her a glass of Perrier water when she is expecting champagne. The real surprise comes when at the bottom of the glass she finds a diamond ring. The only trouble here: our Perrier comes from a 248-foot well. I tried planting a pair of zircon earbobs in a glass of Diet Pepsi, but had it not been for my expertise with the Heimlich maneuver, the poor girl might have choked to death.

Champagne evidently plays a big role in keeping Hollywood people in a romantic state. Another idea for getting out of the marriage rut is to serve hubby the bubbly in bed. If my dear wife served me so much as coffee in bed, I'd spend the rest of the day wondering what she'd been up to.

To rejuvenate hubby's marital excitement, the romance expert advises the wife to change the color of her hair. My wife did that a number of years ago, going from brown to gray. And it didn't exactly have me doing flip-flops. The only time she tried a magic potion to change it artificially, due to an overdose or whatever, was the year we took separate vacations.

"Step out of your usual role and be someone else," to quote the pro. "Anything can be changed, even your name." Oh, yeah? For years my dear wife wanted to change her name to Mrs. Errol Flynn, but it never happened.

The author further advises her readers not to live life secondhand, but to live it firsthand. She says when you see a couple on television being romantic by fireside, "Don't just dreamily stare at the scene. Instead, be romantic by fireside." The catch here is that our heat comes from a floor register. Not too romantic at best. And if the blower should come on, forget it.

Here's another dandy. "If a man puts a red rose next to your bed or a box of chocolates on your pillow, that could give you a big lift." To which I respond, if I catch a man putting a red rose or a box of chocolates anywhere near our bed, he'll get a lift that will make my wife's lift a depression by comparison.

As you can see by now, a couple is not to live "predictable, supermarket lives, with everything prepackaged and prearranged."

The writer illustrates this best by pointing out:

"Anyone who has a lawn can be a prima ballerina." What she suggests may be normal in Tinseltown, of course, but if I ever catch my dear wife dancing on the lawn, I'll have her committed. Unless, that is, she can show me where she has just been punctured by a hornet.

"Dancing," the romance adviser explains, "is a way of communicating with the body." What she has in mind here is ballroom dancing. My wife and I dance occasionally, but I can't recall my body ever saying anything to hers, or vice versa. My favorite compliment for her is the old standby, "You don't sweat much for a fat girl." Whereupon she replies, "You are really light on my feet tonight." Oh, sometimes, if the lights are low and the music soft and slow, she will raise her head from my shoulder and whisper in my ear, "Ouch!" But that's about as romantic as we ever get on the dance floor.

"If in your heart of hearts you see yourself as a horsewoman, learn to ride," is another idea my soul mate wanted to try out. Even though all we have are miniature ponies, if this would put a little zing in her heartstrings, I figured it was at least worth a shot.

Little 28-inch Extract, son of Vanilla, being the liveliest male of the bunch, was selected for this romance-recycling adventure. Getting my dear wife astride the sacrificial beast required a full hour. And by the time I had pulled the little feller's legs out of the ground and helped him into the barn, I couldn't remember why I had been party to such a stunt, much less how it might have affected my wife's romance valves.

Another suggestion of comparable merit is "to swim naked at night in a warm pool." For those who have a warm pool, fine and dandy. Unfortunately, our only warm pool is the result of forgetting to let Brutus, our dog, out at night. We do have a three-foot-square shower stall with a capacity of one adult in which a misdirection in reaching for the soap will bring down the shower caddy. And it takes only one shampoo bottle landing on your foot to disperse any romantic notion you might have for the next three days.

Moving right along: "Have an emergency kit. Candles, fizzy wine, and caviar should always be kept available to make an occasion out of an ordinary day." We have the candle, no problem there, and maybe one out of three isn't so bad. But our only occasion for lighting them is when the power goes off. As for the fizzy wine and caviar, the closest we come to it is a two-liter bottle of Diet Pepsi and a can of water-packed tuna.

Still another love link that hasn't worked out for us has to do with the advice, "The few minutes of peace the two of you spend together by the sea or in the woods will help your marriage, help you to be at ease with each other." To which I say, Ha! The last time my dear wife and I went back to our woods together, we were carrying a two-man/woman crosscut saw, with intentions of cutting a fallen honey locust into wood-stove lengths.

Everything went according to Paul Bunyan for about three cooperative pulls and pushes. At which point she decided that I was jerking her off her feet on purpose. It being a woman's nature, she began trying to do the same to me. This, of course, got my dobber up to the point where the contest ended by her coming out of her boots and draping her body across the log. End of romantic interlude.

"Most of us need the right setting and circumstances to flourish," we are told, "to bring out our romantic selves. When life seems a little dull...take a car ride—anything might happen."

I certainly can't argue with that. We have only to dredge up my dear wife's car ride of last Tuesday for proof that "anything might happen."

Before making her emergency run into Spencer for sleeping pills for her cat, or something equally vital, she romantically asked if she could bring me anything. Like an idiot, I told her she could bring me two 12-foot lengths of gutter for the barn. And for once, she got exactly what I had asked for. As she was coming up the driveway, however, with one end of the gutters resting on top of the back seat and the other end sticking out the front window, the ends sticking out the front window rammed into the tulip tree and shoved the back ends out through the rear window. This, of course, bent the gutters so they're only fit to be used on a silo. And we don't have a silo.

Was that enough romance for one day? Oh, no. Later that day I asked if she would mind moving the remains of her car out of the drive so I could get my car past. Now her key wouldn't turn on the ignition. It has happened before. But this time no matter how hard we jerked on the steering wheel while turning the key, no go.

In desperation, I called Paul Thomas, the No. 1 mechanic on our list, who came out with his wrecker. "Are you sure this is the right key?" he asked. "It doesn't seem to fit the way it should."

Yes, said dear wife. Paul hauled the car in to his garage to replace the ignition.

Upon paying the bill the next day—$72.60 incidentally, which may be incidental to Donald Trump but certainly not to me—Paul said the other key dear wife had given him wouldn't unlock the trunk. Something was obviously rotten in the state of Freedom, Indiana.

Upon broaching the subject to you-know-who at my earliest opportunity, I said, "You must have another set of keys for your car."

"I just threw a set in the junk," replied y-k-w, "but I couldn't find what they were for."

Yep. After pawing through an assortment of cat food cans and dog food cans and a couple of cans for human food, I located the keys. Yep, again. One opened the trunk, and one opened the old ignition, now lying on the back floor. I tell you, romance can hit no higher plane than we enjoyed that night.

In contrast to the far-out ideas this romance writer proposes, one statement I find ultra-conservative. She tells the gals, "Treat marriage as an affair and after 20 years you'll still be a beautiful woman."

Twenty years indeed. Our marriage has survived for 52 years, and my wife is a beautiful woman today. So maybe we have been doing something right, after all.

Chapter 20

THE WRONG STUFF

"The writer's way is rough and lonely," to quote the late Dorothy Parker, "and why would anyone choose it when there are vacancies in more gracious professions, such as cleaning out ferryboats?"

My answer to that is: the writer's way might easily reach the high estate of a ferryboat janitor if only the writer would get a little respect when he is working. We're talking here of distractions from his mate, by the kids, by the kids' kids, even by the dog and the cat. Put them all together, and they spell m-u-r-d-e-r, a word that means like trying to write in a revolving door.

I give my dear wife credit (why not—every store in town has): when an odd job around the house might take me from my desk, she will spare me by doing the odd job all by herself. And an odd job it is. Given a right way and a wrong way to do it, she calls me from my desk because she has opted for the wrong way first.

I refer to the unassembled bookcase she assembled with the unfinished side panels at the top for all to see. The lovely finished ends were resting on the floor, to be enjoyed by the carpet weevils and perhaps a passing termite. I might also mention the stereo cabinet she labored over. The finished side of the back panel faced the wall, where to be admired the set would have to be turned around. Thanks to the glass doors in front, however, the unfinished side showed up nicely. And how can a man concentrate on nouns and verbs until these glaring errors are corrected?

Dear wife claims I tried to even the score by knocking over her lousy passion flower plant. The resulting discussion shot another morning's work. What happened was that her passion flower, perched so smugly on the plastic pedestal I had bought for my unicorn collection, had been lunging at me every time I walked past. This time when it made a pass at me, the poor thing (as I tried to explain) must have lost its balance. Just because the pot happened to strike my elbow on the way down, dear wife took it as evidence that I had nudged it off its perch. Just between you and me, however, that is one plant down and, at last count, 46 to go.

Now this isn't to imply that my dear wife is vindictive, but the next day, going into the kitchen for a decaffeinated-coffee break, I found her shaving the

NOTHING SERIOUS, I HOPE

carrots with my one and only razor. Rising up on my hind legs, I remarked that my mother had always had good luck scraping carrots with a knife. I further politely suggested that if she preferred shaving to scraping, she could use her own confounded razor. A narrowing of her nostrils and a little more cleave in her cleavage told me it would be wise to abandon the subject right there. She, on the other hand, was more than willing to continue. She informed me that her razor had been missing ever since I had scraped the flaking paint off the board fence. She further declaimed that if a he-man razor couldn't take a little scraping, then it was high time the Gillette people made one that would. And she demanded to know where I kept my blades—this one was pretty well shot. At which point, to my credit, I slammed nothing but the front door.

Maybe I'm too compassionate—I don't know. But I can't seem to concentrate when my marital relationship borders on a "Mr." and "Mrs." basis. One thorn in our marital flesh involves my dear wife's cat. I call her Lump. (The cat, that is. I haven't called my dear wife Lump since—I believe it was just before I got my upper partial.)

Anyway, my dear wife buys liver chunks for my dog, Brutus. Doing him a favor, you think? In a pig's eye. Brutus prefers beef chunks. It's her gluttonous cat that likes liver chunks for dessert after a hearty meal of Crunchie Wunchies, or whatever. The last time I caught her pampered pussy elbowing my dog away from his dish, my foot gently eased the arrogant beast ten feet or more over to her own dish. My reward for this justifiable act was freedom to get my own meals for the next two days.

After my bitter half leaves on her daily shopping spree to get sleeping pills for her cat or something equally vital, I can then begin putting words between punctuation marks, right? Wrong. This woman with whom I joined my plight in the trough of holy wedlock, or however that goes, doesn't know an air filter from a box of Shredded Wheat when it comes to cars. Consequently, when her car konks out on the highway, she looks up a telephone instead of looking under the hood. And does she call a mechanic? Don't be silly! Isn't old hubby at home doing nothing but staring at a blank sheet of paper in his typewriter?

"It went kawhing...kawhang...kawhung...and quit," she sniffled into the phone on this last (make that latest—heaven and I know it won't be the last) occurrence.

From this precise description I should have pinpointed the trouble right off, of course. But I had to let a $30-an-hour serviceman interpret "kawhing, kawhang, kawhung" as caused by buckeyes from our backyard tree. Thirty-eight, by actual count, or about a buck apiece, which some inconsiderate little varmint had stored in the air filter by squeezing itself up the air hose. So now the chore of checking the air filter for foreign matter before my mate takes off is added to my daily schedule.

After the most recent assault on my think buds (out of the blue she said, "By the way, your dog is senile"), I suggested I might as well close the lid on my old Remington Noiseless and just retire.

"From what?" came her ready response.

Come to think of it, in all the years I have been secluding myself in this book-lined pigeonhole—which I refer to on my tax form as a home office—I can't remember dear wife's ever being curious about what went on in here. The only reason she comes in is to throw a sheet over me if we're having company. To let her read about her foibles I reveal from time to time would be about as rewarding as exploring a wall socket with a wet finger.

Our kids, however, never took after my dear wife. They took after me—at every possible opportunity. I'm talking about their routing their train tracks around my desk and between my feet. I'm talking about their turning my desk into an intensive care unit for everything from a barbecued butterfly removed from the car grille to a toad one hop short of escaping the mower. I'm talking about their sticking bubble gum on my typewriter keys and their playing tiddlywinks with my paper clips.

When the last tiddlywinker had finally left home for college, I exhaled for the first time in decades and said to myself (I was talking a lot to myself by then): That is that. Somehow I had over-overlooked the possibility of our kids eventually having kids of their own.

So once more my pigeonhole has been mined with toys on wheels that take me regularly from desk to filing cabinet in nothing flat. And I do mean flat. If I shoot past the filing cabinet, as I did once, my next stopping point is the door casing. But I had to be told about this incident—I was not myself at the time. Or for some time afterward. The only time this rabble is quiet is when they are busily drawing and coloring unidentifiable objects on page after page after page of my legal pads, priced at 75 cents per. But how can I clamp down on the little prodigals when they so adoringly identify their unidentifiable objects as me?

Moreover, if moreover is necessary, they even outdo their parents when it comes to performing mouth-to-bill resuscitation on a defrocked cardinal or a mourning dove that isn't kidding. I give you the recent case of a box turtle as a prime example.

How recently the corpse had been a box turtle I can only speculate, because only the shell remained. Its being reduced to only a shell of its former self (which proves the state to which I have now been reduced), however, would in no way detract from the solemnity of its funeral, to which I had been solemnly invited.

Per instructions, I left my desk, poised pen still in hand, and stood at the kitchen door while the hastily recruited mourners, faces white with rampant dabs of talcum, filed past. On a sofa cushion, supported by four sniveling pallbearers, lay the turtle's remains. With much effort, as the procession shuffled past me on the way to the peony-bed burial ground, I managed to keep my composure, until on signal the snivelers broke into that most mournful of all dirges: "Here comes the bride."

I tell you, it takes a writer with greater concentrative powers than I possess to go back to work after a soul wrencher of that magnitude.

Lastly—that'll be the day—there's our telephone answering service. Me, I can be at my desk, in the shower, or attending a turtle funeral—if the phone rings, it's automatic for my dear wife to yell, "Telephone!" I could be half a mile down the road, and she'd drive down to tell me the phone is ringing. And nine times out of ten it will be one of her quilting buddies asking me to relay the message that the Tuesday session has been canceled because Bertha can't find her needle.

One of these days when she yells, "Telephone!" I'm going to shoot from the lip and yell back. "So why don't you answer it?"

On second thought, maybe I won't. With all these interruptions reducing my output, right now I can't afford a new upper partial.

Chapter 21

SOMETHING TO BARK ABOUT

"I didn't know whether it *was* safe to get out of the car or not," the census taker chirped. "I saw your sign at the end of the driveway: 'Beware of M.G. Stoddard.'"

After she had finished prying into how many bathrooms we had in our little termite picnic shelter and such, I walked down the drive to see if she was just being cute. No, by golly, she was right. The "Dog" had disappeared from the sign, and the "Beware of" led directly to the wooden letters of my name beneath it. My dear wife was quick to express an opinion that the sign made sense as it stood. She was, I'm sure, referring to the fact that 12-year-old Brutus no longer could detect a prowler if one stepped on his tail, much less hear a car coming up the drive.

Nevertheless, in hopes of fooling some of the people some of the time, I bought a new "Beware of Dog" sign and, armed with sign, hammer, and five nails (one to drop in the long grass below the sign), I headed for the post at the foot of the drive. On the way, thinking all the time, I thought, *I'll switch the nails from my right-hand coat pocket to the left-hand coat pocket because I'll be hammering with my right hand, and it will be difficult to put that hand into my coat pocket to get the nails while it's holding the hammer.* Got that? Maybe you'd better go over it again.

Making the switch while wearing gloves wasn't easy, but I managed it. Only to find upon arriving at the post that my left-hand coat pocket didn't possess a bottom. I looked up and down the drive until my eyeballs bulged, but no nails. My left front tire, however, had no trouble picking up the first two that same day. I'm sure the other three will turn up shortly by the same means. If I'd only thought of this sooner, it would have saved a lot of looking.

It's no wonder that Lump, our cat, is the only thing around here that purrs. My dear wife hums, Brutus whines, and I—so it is said—bark. If that is true, at least I have plenty to bark about.

I've just come down with a bad case of smut from stacking bales of straw around our fuel-oil tank. Dear wife, a retired R.N., says I am crazy. "It's nothing but a mild touch of leprosy" was her diagnosis, which she thought was real funny. It would serve her right if that's what it turns out to be.

I'm also having trouble shaving because of fruit flies fogging the mirror. Which raises the question of whether we keep fruit in the bathroom. The answer is no. It's got to be that jug of strawberry cologne one of the grandsons bestowed upon his doting grandmother this past Christmas.

In hopes of no longer having to repeat everything I say, I took advantage of this same gift-giving occasion to surprise my dear wife with a hearing aid. She won't wear it because she says it doesn't fit. I thought all ears were the same size. Except for the outside flaps, of course.

This place seemed to be a breeding ground for controversy. Before the ground froze this winter, I asked dear wife to lay aside *Hearts Aflame,* her complete library, and help me replace three chewed-up wooden fence posts with steel posts, which, I hoped, would offer the termites more of a challenge. How trippingly the names of other duos come off the tongue: Abbott and Costello, Martin and Lewis, Gilbert and Sullivan, corned beef and cabbage. Now try Lois and Maynard. Sort of sticks in your throat, right? And for good reason. (Excuse me—her cat just dipped its tail in my coffee.)

To decide which of us would hold the post and which would mount the stepladder with the sledge hammer to drive the post into the ground, I took a poll. And her answer was, I'll hold the post, thank you."

I said, "O.K., steady the ladder."

She said, "I can't steady the ladder and hold the post too. What do you think I am?"

Here I'd been waiting years for this opening, and whatd'ya know, folks, I lost my nerve. So I had scaled halfway up the ladder, at which point, in scaling ladders while carrying sledge hammers, one can drop the sledge hammer on his foot or not. It's optional. I usually do. And I did. So I scaled back down the ladder, and after regaining my power of speech, I said, "Would it be convenient, light of my life, to hold the ladder instead of the post until I have arrived safely at the step from which I can apply the sledge hammer to the confounded post?"

Even employing that strategy, I defy any man, including Schwarzenegger himself, to stand on a ladder holding a 16-pound sledge hammer and apply it to the top of a post that a woman is waving around like a drum major's baton. So naturally I missed completely, and the velocity of my swing sent me sailing over the fence. Had it not been for landing in a clump of thorn bushes, I might have been hurt.

"Why couldn't you hold it steady?" I yelled up at her.

"Why couldn't you hit where I held it?" was her rejoinder. And when my dear wife rejoins, it's just as well not to pursue the matter further. The last such exchange ended with her statement that one more word and I'd be parking for the next two weeks in places reserved for the handicapped. Sometimes that woman is tougher than her pot roasts.

Maynard Good Stoddard

Our efforts to work together are not always this serious, of course. They can actually be funny. Funny to one of us, anyway. Her helping me to install a new blade in my bow saw would be a fair illustration. All I wanted her to do was line up one of the two holes in the end of the blade and hook it over this little peg when I pushed down on the metal bow, which would require every muscle, sinew, and tendon on my whole united body. And I was right in the middle of this superhuman effort...when she began to giggle. Giggle and jiggle. And when that woman begins to jiggle, you can just forget it.

"What's so funny?" I wheezed.

"The holes keep going past the peg—there goes one now," she screamed. Oh, how funny! Here my small intestine was practically tied in a granny knot from exertion, and she was having a ball. I finally gave up and took advantage of my adrenaline flow to retire to the patio and push the bow down myself, although my clavicle will never be the same.

In way of apology, the next day dear wife drove into Spencer and charged a ceiling fan to my account at the hardware store. She had been expecting one for Christmas, instead of the hearing aid. And did she want it put in the living room, where it would make a little sense? Don't be silly. It was going in the kitchen, presumably to cool the tasting samples of tuna hash or whatever she was throwing together for the evening mess.

And of course, to install the thing she had to call Martin Morton—or is it Morton Martin? I could look it up on one of his bills. Lord knows we've got enough of them lying around.

Upon arriving home the next night, I noticed that the yard could have served for no man's land in a war movie. We're talking here of trenches, bunkers, foxholes, the whole business. When I saw the lengths of pipe lying around, I rushed in to embrace my surprised wife. "You went out to bury the garbage and struck oil!" I joyously cried. "Good girl!"

She said, "Don't be silly. After Martin got the fan up, I showed him the leak under the sink." She was referring to a drip of no consequence I had already taken care of by placing a plastic bucket under it. If we remembered to dump the bucket three times during the day and three times during the night, it was, as I say, of no consequence.

"So how did that rip our yard asunder?" was my pertinent question.

The answer was that in checking, Martin, or Morton, had discovered that not only was our drainage pipe too small, but even what we had had been thoroughly plugged with roots from the French lilac.

"So when is he coming back?" was pertinent question No.2.

"He isn't."

"He whatn't?"

"I told him you could finish it. It'll save hiring him for another day."

A day, she said. I worked at the project practically full-time for a week. To be honest, however—but I wouldn't want this to go any further—it wouldn't have taken so long if only I'd remembered to lay the pipe before filling in the trenches. Some men for piping and some for typing, as I tried to explain to dear wife while she was draining my blisters into a pot of African violets.

In review, what concerns me most is that the woman is only a heartbeat away from taking over this whole shebang. Then she'll probably marry some handkissing vulture who'll squander our whole estate in less than two weeks.

Maybe instead of a will I'll leave a won't. She won't get but half. The other half I'll split between Tom, our mechanic at Algood's Chevrolet, and Morton Martin—in case the handkisser is no more adept at repairing stuff than I am.

Chapter 22

DO YOU TAKE THIS MAN?

AND HOW!

It is said that a man who promises to move heaven and earth for his bride is the same man who later growls when he's asked to move the davenport.

There are any number of reasons for this about-face. Take my case, if you have a strong stomach.

At the exhilarating age of 24 I was sailing through life free as a bird on the wing. New car. Money in the bank. Countenance unlined. Dating any number of girls. Then, on December 7, 1941 (or was that the day the Japanese bombed Pearl Harbor? I get the two dates confused), I took this particular girl to a Chinese restaurant for her birthday. And the rest is history, as they say.

Where I made my mistake was in asking how she liked her rice, boiled or fried. And she said, "Thrown."

Before I could come up with a logical way out, we were standing before a justice of the peace (certainly a misnomer for a guy who started all this ruckus), and the girl was answering yes, she would take this man.

Well, I can say this for her: she has certainly done a good job of it.

As things stand now, my wings have been clipped, my car is an early '77, the money that comes in goes out as though it had been last handled by lepers, and my face is wrinkled to the point I am obliged to shave with a potato peeler.

Actually, I didn't begin to fall apart until making my first sale—a poem bought by *Liberty* magazine for $20. And now that my literary career had been firmly established, in the words of my bride—why not borrow $1,500 to put with the $20, buy a house trailer, and take off for Florida? There I would make Hemingway's efforts, by comparison, read more like a sixth grader's "What I Did on My Summer Vacation." And you know something, folks, I fell for it.

And did so well, believe it or not, that in a matter of only four months we had to sell the car. Either that or give up the acquired habit of eating. We would come close enough even then, as it turned out.

My stomach rumbles were already beginning to be heard above the surf, in fact, when the mailman delivered, along with his normal cargo of rejected manuscripts, a beautiful blue envelope from *Extension* magazine. I kept reading the letter over and over. No joke "Do You Mind if I Breathe" had been accepted—for the lifesaving sum of $150.

And we were off again. This time in a Velie housecar.

I had stumbled upon this relic in the jungle behind the trailer park. After the car's six years of hibernation, vines had taken up residence in all four cylinders. But what I didn't know then was that even in its heyday the car had rightfully acquired the slogan "If the hood is up, it's a Velie."

No matter. Now that we again had wheels, and because you-know-who had always wanted to visit Mexico City, what was to stop us? A list of what was to stop us would easily run to book length.

Let's just say that I was under "The Thing," as it came to be called, more than I was in it. Upon finally reaching New Orleans, by the skin of my knuckles and a vote of one to one, I turned north toward home, mother, apple pie, the American flag, and the convenience of being able to borrow a few bucks when necessary. Little did I know we were heading for an abandoned nine-room farmhouse near the tidy Germantown of Frankenmuth, Michigan.

When I say abandoned, I'm talking about baled hay stored in the living room. I'm talking about doors that wouldn't close until I had sawed a hunk off the bottom—in one case a hunk so generous, after the third try, that the cat enjoyed the convenience of going in and out without having to ask. I'm talking about a flooded cellar I had promised my dear wife I would drain into the frog pond. Through a miscalculation the frog pond drained into the cellar. For my pains I received another 150 bucks for an article, "How I Converted an Old Farmhouse into a Shambles."

After we went through a lengthy dry spell, including six healing years in a snug Indianapolis apartment, this woman got the urge to take over our current termite condo atop one of Sweet Owen County's rolling hills that stop rolling just short of Freedom, (Indiana, of course), where I have suffered in silence long enough.

Upon moving to any new location, the female gender has this gene which immediately begins to nag her that nothing is in the right place—including the landscape. I refer, in this case, to the two acres (perhaps more, but I don't want to risk exaggeration) overgrown with sassafras, locust sapling, briar bushes, wild grape, and—you name it, it was there. This woman right off came up with the idea that God had intended this jungle to be a lawn. A wild animal perserve, yes. But a lawn!

The fact that all this flora had been anchored on a slope that would have challenged a mountain goat was inconsequential. As for the fact that this could also be the favorite breeding ground for copperheads, that could only help to hurry the project along.

So while I'm out there for the next four months converting this wilderness into mowable condition, this woman is in the house happily hemming drapes and hanging lethal crock pots from the ceiling. And after ripping the last briar-bush tendril off my aching back, did I happily begin mowing the so-called lawn? Have you ever tried to stay aboard a riding mower while negotiating a 40-degree slope? If so, then you know that your full concentration is required just to keep from ending up with a hot Briggs and Stratton in your lap. So when three jet aircraft from the National Guard at Terre Haute come roaring over, evidently using my mower as a marker, I respond like any sensible man certain his mower is exploding—I jump off and run for my life. I am now on my fourth mower since moving here. They sure don't last long going downhill on their own.

This woman had also concluded that God had not arranged the rocks in their proper order. Instead of forming a path from the carport-shed to the house, He had buried them in the creek bed winding through the woods. And who was nominated to correct the divine error? Right. And was the path to conform to the shortest distance between two points? Don't be silly. The boulders being plentiful and the exercise doing me good, the path would go the scenic route—along the row of blue spruce, then winding artistically around to the patio step. Nothing could better reveal my mental state by the time I had lugged up the last one of those suckers and put it in place than the inscription it now bears: "In God We Truss."

Giving credit where credit is questionable, this woman who took me does undertake some of her brainstorms all by herself—for example, installing the homemade bird feeder, made at home by John, my brother-in-law. Why he gave it to us, I don't know. I never did anything to him.

But not to worry. My dear wife would paint the bird feeder, nail it to a two-by-four, and anchor the two-by-four in the ground just off the patio. And she actually did paint it. All well and good. Except she used my best paintbrush, which I later found stuck in a Jiffy peanut jar from which the turpentine had evaporated. The brush is now good for nothing but pounding the meat for Swiss steak.

And she did come up from the barn dragging a ten-foot two-by-four all by herself. (What it had been supporting there I'll know soon enough.) After making sure she had my full attention, she began digging a hole with that little scoop she likes to use for potting geraniums.

I calculated that unless she buried at least six feet of the two-by-four (which at the rate she was going wouldn't be covered until the birds in our area had become extinct), we would have to use a stepladder to put in the seeds. So I—as I'm sure she had calculated—took over. Sawed four feet off the two-by-four, located the posthole diggers, dug through two feet of elm-tree roots and sandstone, dropped in the two-by-four, nailed on the bird feeder, and staggered into the house. She was at her sewing machine. She hummed happily as she hemmed another drape.

I am now preparing a manuscript to be titled "Fiddler on the Roof." I have fiddled away more time on the roof of this termite tabernacle than I have on the couch. In the Indianapolis apartment we occupied while this woman was formulating plans for another attack on rural America, I had only to call Maintenance if the roof leaked. Here, I *am* Maintenance. And I am on duty 24 or more hours a day.

The tar I have already spread on the roof would easily resurface our driveway. How the roof can support it is a miracle. I quit adding to it the day the temp hit 94. Tar began dripping off the roof onto her four-o'clocks, and she became a bit testy because their blooming hours went from Eastern Standard to Mountain time.

My final day on the roof, I stood so long in one place that, upon being called for lunch, I discovered that my shoes were stuck. Not keen about coming out of them and walking across a sea of hot tar in my socks, I had my lunch brought up the ladder and served to me on a broom. From the gawking of the neighbors driving past, you'd have thought they had never seen anyone eating lunch from a broom on the roof of his house.

I had to wait until after sunset for the tar to cool to the point I could walk across in my socks. My shoes are still up there.

Well, if you can't beat 'em, join 'em, as the saying goes. So instead of trying to keep the water out, I did the next best thing—I dealt with it after it came in. I'm talking about suspending a gutter from the kitchen ceiling beneath the most copious drips and running the downspout into the sink. It was a bailing-wire-mechanic's masterpiece, if you overlook losing all that sink space plus the view through the kitchen window. But it worked beautifully.

Yet how true it is: you can't please some of the people any of the time. And because of one such people, our waterbed stayed frozen cold until the "contraption," as it was so rudely labeled, had been dismantled.

Will you take this man, indeed!

Chapter 23

THE REEL CHALLENGE

Although "togetherness" today rates right up there in popularity with the rummage sale at a fish market, there are weekends when husband wife are thrown together with no delicate way of avoiding it. So when this circumstance occurred with my own dear wife and me on a recent ill-starred weekend, I suggested that since we would be together anyway, we might better be together fishing than sitting in front of the TV having our eyes crossed.

For sheer brilliance, the idea turned out to be on a par with playing leapfrog with a porcupine.

Not that I am placing all the blame on the other party. From overt elevations of the nose whenever I had come home from stag fishing galas, I was aware that Lois was no Mrs. Izaak Walton. But as I hadn't enjoyed a gala since leaving the lakes of Michigan for the hinterland of Indiana, neither caution nor common sense was going to interfere.

In fact, I even experienced a fleeting moment of optimism while rushing home on Friday afternoon to pick up the baggage, most of which awaited me on the front porch. There was also a note glued to the cork grip of my casting rod informing me that the writer could be picked up at the beauty parlor. By the time we then stopped at the laundry ("You surely didn't expect me to go in dirty clothes!") and made a detour to her mother's house to drop off an African Violet convalescing from a touch of neglect, we reached the cottage at Lake Wawasee too late for anything but bullheading. And I'd sooner listen to a woman play gin rummy than try to remove a hook from a bullhead. But not much sooner.

Saturday morning. Breakfast laid out on the table. Can opener neatly laid out beside it. But no Lois. A quick stumble to the window revealed ideal conditions: gentle breeze from the west (when fish bite the best) ruffling the lake, fish jumping in joyful anticipation of a boat ride, kids on the dock hauling out keepers.

Jerking my jogging shorts on over my pajamas and grabbing my rod and tackle box, I dashed out the door, stopping to reach under the front steps where I had carelessly tossed the oars the night before. Gone.

By the time I had sprinted to the end of the dock, Lois was more than a stone's throw offshore (I'm just guessing at this, as there wasn't a stone to be found).

"Come back and get me!" I shouted, like a man watching his wife pull away with the last available boat—which it was.

"After I pick a bouquet of water lilies," she yelled back.
"Water lil—! Holy mackerel, woman, don't you see those fish jumping!"
Yes, she saw them. She also saw that I was still in my pajamas...and she bet I hadn't shaved...and had I eaten?
Not until the wind had shifted to due north and was gusting the shingles off the outside plumbing did she return with a handful of limp water lilies. I found them later struggling for survival on the gin-rummy table. The evening turned uncommonly cool.
By morning, waves were washing over the dock, fish flies lay on the water thick enough to clog a motor. But thanks to Lois's magnanimous announcement that "this is *your day—and you* are going fishing, come hell or high water" (we would have both), I was dressed, fed, shaved and bailing out the boat at approximately 5:30 a.m.
By 6:15, I had managed to lighten the boat to the point where only every third or fourth wave was breaking over us. The boat and me, that is. Lois was bustling about, loading the vital supplies. An hour later, she had the boat wallowing under pillows, knitting equipment, suntan lotion, portable TV, first-aid kit, cooler, camera, picnic basket, box of chocolates, insect spray, three back issues of the *Reader's Digest,* binoculars, writing paper, folding chair and a pair of rubber gloves (don't ask—I didn't). At the last minute I remembered my rod and tackle box.

Halfway across the lake, the oars making contact with foam on the wave tops only, I had to turn back. She had forgotten her purse.
As midday was now approaching, I proposed anchoring at the nearest weed bed and satisfying my fishing lust with a few under-sized bluegills. No way. This was *my* day, and we would go where the woman who rented us the cottage said her nephew's cousin caught that 20-pound pike six years ago on a bent pin.
"But big fish don't hit in the middle of the day," I explained.
"That's nonsense!" she explained back, trying to capture a chocolate in the throes of a bobbing boat. "They have to eat lunch the same as everyone else does."
Encouraged by this sound reasoning, I rowed to the place where the nephew's cousin or cousin's nephew...etc., and half-heartedly looped a red-and-white daredevil toward a patch of lily pads. I'm not even sure it hit the water before that tremendous splash and the tip of my rod bent nearly to the reel, which began to sing as it hadn't sung in years.

"Why don't you either oil that thing or put it up!" Lois groaned, sweeping my gear off the center seat and replacing it with the picnic basket. "You know screeching always makes my flesh crawl!"

"If it would crawl out of the boat for a minute, maybe I could get this fish to crawl in," I panted. Then added, to my instant regret, "...gotta keep it away from that anchor rope!"

"Well, why didn't you say so!" chided my fishing companion, burrowing into her stack of junk.

Then that lovely thing (the fish) came alongside—for one brief but golden moment, just long enough for my little goaltender to jab it away with her umbrella. Not until I coaxed it back the third time was she to uncover the landing net.

"Do I stick the mesh part into the water or hold it out so you can slip the fish into it?"

I told her to stick the mesh part into the water, in front of and slightly below the fish, *when I gave the word!*

A final flurry (from the fish), and then, with an inflection I hadn't used since our honeymoon, I breathed, *"Now!"* Considering this was her first time at handling the net, I suppose she didn't do too poorly—the cooler, a seat cushion and my tackle box all in that one scoop. She even had that pike hanging on the outside for a full second. But when the monster let my camera settle out of sight without snapping it up and choking to death, my last hope vanished.

Not until I was tying up back at the dock did we engage in any in-depth conversation. And then it was only because a bass had clamped on the piece of red wool yarn she had draped over a hook to trail behind the boat.

"Play it!" I screamed, leaping to clear the net.

"Play it, my foot!" she retorted. And a second later this large mouth (the fish) bounced into the boat, where Lois belted it with her purse.

It's not that I am opposed to the ancient ideal of man-and-woman togetherness. But there's a time and a place for everything. And the place is *not* beyond the waterline.

Chapter 24

SPACED OUT

We have a coat closet just off the patio door. By actual account, it contains 17 coats and 15 1/2 coat hangers. One of the plastic hangers has lost a shoulder on the right side—or left side, depending on which way you hook it over the rod. Fifteen of the coats belong to my dear wife; two are mine.

I have a spring-fall coat and winter coat. My winter coat is eight years old. The buttons on my spring-fall coat are made of mica, the forerunner of plastic. The last time I wore it, an elderly gentleman said he hadn't seen buttons like that in 30 years. It would probably take a carbon-14 test to determine the age of the thing. Two of Lois' coats still carry the price tags.

Her coats occupy the 15 whole hangers. By running one sleeve of my spring-fall coat over the shoulder of the half hanger and wrapping the other sleeve around the hook, the coat will stay up for, oh, sometimes as long as five minutes.

My winter coat I hang over the handle of the vacuum cleaner. This keeps most of it off the floor but leaves a hummock in the back that has people on the street looking at me as if they think my spinal column might have slipped its mooring and punched through my skin.

At spring housecleaning time, which came late this year, Lois said, "We've just got to get rid of some of these coats!"
I, in my naivete, replied, "I'm all for that."
She immediately plunged in and, after a morning of pawing and sorting and mumbling, took my spring-fall coat to the rummage sale at the Freedom fire hall.
If the problem were confined to the coat closet, I wouldn't bring it up. But pick any area in the house Go ahead, pick any area—I'll wait.
Our clothes closets? Good choice.
Here, I have good news and bad news. The good news is, we have separate closets. The bad news—they connect. From our original starting pointing of 50-50, her clothes now extend to a full three-quarters of the space; my remnants are scrunched up at the far end of what was once my half. President Reagan would have to take but one look at the scene to declare it a disaster area eligible for a low-interest loan (which we could use).
The financial outlay to support the habit of this clothesaholic I married is one thing. Another is the risk it presents to life, limb, and the top of the head. Open a closet door, and whammo!—clothes she hasn't worn since her baby fat returned

spring out with a great sigh of relief. I barely emerge from this deluge before a stack of folding chairs begins unfolding on my shins. And as I bend over and try to figure out how to refold the blasted things, I find my head is invariably lined up just right to stop her overloaded shoetree from crashing to the floor.

You could as well have picked any area in the house—the problem is the same. My dear wife, you see, is a collector of—well, to be fair, let's call it junk. You've probably heard of Ringwald's Law of Household Geometry: "Any horizontal surface is soon piled up." I don't know where Ringwald did his research, but any one of our rooms would have served as an ideal site. I propose (if Ringwald wouldn't mind) an amendment to his law: "Surfaces pile up in direct proportion to the number of flea markets, garage sales, and farm auctions within a 50-mile radius."

I have done my best to slow this transfer of someone else' castoffs to our own collection point: For a recent farm auction I made her promise she would keep her hands in her pockets during the bidding. She said she would only watch. So I put the wires back on the spark plugs and drove 27 miles over back roads in the rain so my little spectator could see the first heirloom go up for sale.

To her credit, she kept her word about keeping her hands in her pockets. She got the winning bid—on the croquet set with five balls and one mallet, the box of textbooks all in French, the 2'x5' mirror molting its quicksilver, and the framed photo of someone named George waving from a fire tower on Big Bear Mountain on April 14, 1927—by winking at the auctioneer. And after I positioned myself in front of her, she added a dilapidated wren condo, a carton of udder salve she mistook for neutral shoe polish, and a cracked bust of Millard Fillmore—by throwing her leg in the air.

Not only do I have to load and unload this crud and usually add another rip to the car's upholstery, but hours later I find it usurping the space normally reserved for essentials. One incident comes to mind—perhaps because it occurred about an hour ago. In the orchard counting my crop of four Bartlett pears, I noticed that a convention of bagworms had convened on an upper limb. Dashing into the house, I grabbed the blowtorch from the top of the refrigerator and went out to adjourn the convention. Ten minutes later, I came back to find Millard Fillmore in the vacated place looking smugly down at me.

I know what you girls are thinking: "Why don't you store your big, fat blowtorch out in the shed where it belongs?" That shows how little you know about conditions in the shed, built only three years ago to shelter those items too awkward to maneuver through the kitchen door. I refer to such items as the Rototiller, the snow blower, some garden tools, my riding mower, her self-propelled mowers—stuff like that. Today, the shed looks like an uncataloged annex to the Smithsonian.

Take just her self-propelleds...Please. While I've been nursing one riding mower for the past six years, she has gone through three self-propelleds. And they lie in wait in various stages of disrepair to break the leg of anyone trying to get his riding mower through the maze.

One of these junkers self-propelled itself over a stump in the barnyard after it got away from her coming downhill. The next one she banked off the security-light pole. While she checked for broken fingernails, the contraption proceeded to mow the stones down one track of the driveway. Although she still operates the third mower, a toothless sheep could gum the grass about as well, due to close encounters with the rock gardens (see below).

Throw the other two wrecks away? She won't hear of it. For me to have access to my mower, snow blower, etc., nothing would be left in the way but the six bales of straw she is going to mulch her strawberry patch with, already in the seed-catalog stage; a rubber tree that died in her arms one night after serving as a nail-sharpening post for the cat, but that she still fertilizes with what must be—judging from the cost—aardvark droppings; and the sofa, retired four years ago, whose availability has spread to every mice colony in sweet Owen County.

By comparison, getting to my garden tools is a breeze. All I have to do is walk the length of the sofa, step from one junk mower to the next, then climb to the top of the six bales of straw. From this vantage point, I can usually spot the tool I'm after just inside the door, where she leaves everything instead of putting it on its proper wall bracket.

That's another thing...but it'll have to wait.

Three years ago Lois began drumming into my ears that our marriage would stand a better chance of survival if I would have the front porch enclosed.

No sooner said than done—give or take a year or two—I finally gave in for two reasons. Not only would giving in save wear and tear on my eardrums, but her plans called for 12 windows with a foot-wide ledge to run the full length beneath. In my innocence, I figured that after a hard day of nouning and verbing the ledge would be ideal for sitting with my feet propped up as I looked out over the valley and the lights of Freedom began to illumine the evening sky. The ledge would also be just the place for hedge trimmers, mole traps, Weed Eaters, pruning shears, birdseed, and other staples I use around the house. *(Around* the house, not *in* the house.)

Feel free to stop by anytime and take a look. If you can find a peephole big enough to spot a romantic firefly in the evening sky, you're doing better than I am. As for the ledge, the entire length is crammed with odds and ends, the odds running about 10 to 1 over the ends. Wherever this stuff doesn't snuff out the view, my wife has strategically placed macrame flora (some of which, if you'll forgive me, reaches clear to the floor-a).

After writing off this project as a bad investment, I approached Lois one morning in a suppliant position (she didn't know it was the result of having dug out an elm-tree stump the day before) and said, "If you don't mind [an approach I highly recommend], I'd like to put up a couple of shelves in the kitchen."

"Great idea!" she responded, with an enthusiasm I misinterpreted completely. Otherwise I wouldn't have spent seven long evenings, to say nothing of blood, sweat, and assorted blisters, measuring, sawing, remeasuring, resawing, and installing two shelves that still came to inches short of filling the space between wall and cupboards.

What had kept my blood flowing, my sweat dripping, and my blisters accumulating was the happy thought of no more walking 50 feet through the rain to get the pipe wrench from the shed after using a wire coat hanger (from one of her coats) to unplug the sink. The shelves would also hold the plastic bucket I always put under the pipe connection after using the wrench. I would keep the drill there for drilling a hole in the floor under the sink should she get tired of mopping up after the bucket overflows.

On the shelves I would keep Brutus' Frisbee...and the little red lantern I bought at Morgan's auction that I haven't yet found a globe for...and the ball of binder twine I used to bind my *Time, Newsweek,* and *U.S. News & World Report* magazines.

And it worked out just the way I'd planned—from Saturday afternoon clear through Monday. Tuesday night I came home to find my treasures blocking the door to the shed.
"How come my treasures from the shelves are blocking the door to the shed?" I demanded, leaving my coat on in case I had to drive back to Spencer for dinner.
"Because those awful things belong out there," she replied. "I left the stuff out because I thought you'd want to arrange it yourself. Kitchen shelves are for kitchen items."
Still in my coat—a wise decision—I went in to check the kitchen items now occupying the shelves. I found an electric can opener lying on its back ("It doesn't work any more standing up"), a cup rack designed to save space resting on a 14-inch ceramic plate, and a 12-cup coffee urn last used on Thanksgiving Day 1979. The rest of that shelf was taken up by pots of dangling ivy and the all-important canister set. One canister contained a single marshmallow, and another

houses the manual for the sewing machine we gave to our daughter Shari three years ago.

Shelf No. 2, from what little I could see of shelf No. 2 through the ivy hanging from shelf No. 1, contained the miniature rake and shovel I had given her as a peace offering the time I watered the flowers in her rock garden with water left over from a concrete-patching job on the patio. (I remember we had quite a difference of opinion over whether cemented flowers were any worse than those plastic jobs she usually finds in the bottom of the boxes she gets for a 50-cents bid at auctions). I also spotted the walkie-talkie set I gave her and gave up on because you-know-who talkied more than she walkied.

Other kitchen items included three bottles of cat mange cure, a bottle of cat ear-mite medicine, a box of dry cat food, and three cans of cat food her finicky cat wouldn't touch when she lived here, which was three months ago.

"She could come back at any time," Lois explained, in answer to my raised eyebrow.

"So could Amelia Earhart," I pointed out. I ate dinner at the OV Restaurant in Spencer.

As mentioned, we have what is called a root cellar. It is called a root cellar because there a gardener is supposed to store his crop of roots: carrots, peanuts, rutabagas, onions, stuff like that—for the winter. If it were meant to be a place to store boxes of flea market coats that can't be squeezed into the closet, it would have been called a coat cellar, I keep pointing out. And my roots wouldn't have to be stored under the bed, where they begin to sprout two weeks later, I also mention.

Our yard is the last straw. And I do mean straw. Where other people have grass, we have a no man's land of mole tunnels, mole high-rises, and dog excavations made trying to dig them out. This is the law of nature. But where grass does somehow manage to grow, we immediately have rock gardens—well named, I might add. In other yards flowers relieve the monotony of these slag heaps. Not here. If it weren't for the ability of weeds to push up through the billiard-ball clay that passes for topsoil on our hilltop estate, all my dear wife's landscaping would come to naught.

Speaking of which: Six years ago the reforestation people of our Hoosier state advertised their baby pine seedlings for sale, not by a reasonable dozen, or even a halfway-sensible 25, but by a ridiculous 100. And guess who jumped on the offer to the tune of 200? Right.

To her astonishment, they survived. Today, those babies are 20 feet high and interlaced. They make it necessary for me to climb the fence and walk through Abrell's pasture to get from the house to the garden. Only an act of God will keep the limbs from entering our house in another two years. The roots have already strangled our kitchen drain. As for any chance of daylight coming through the living-room picture window that cost $166 to install, forget it. I might as well have painted the thing black in one swell foop.

I'd better not go on. It's not good for a man of my years to get worked up to the point that his pulse can be picked up on the Richter scale.

Chapter 25

POWER WALK

"Louis Sullivan and his wife power walk three miles a day," I said to my own dear wife through a hole in the morning paper where I had clipped the address of Credit Cards Anonymous.

To no surprise, she recognized Dr. Sullivan as our popular Secretary of Health and Human Services. What surprised me was that she had been listening. And for surprise number two, she peeked through the hole and said, "Why don't we give it a shot?" and even rambled on, something about my excess weight, my blood pressure, my cholesterol, and my bad temper.

What I had in mind, of course, was doing something about the persistence of her own baby fat. I also had noticed that Brutus, my dog, had cut his exercise regimen from jumping fences to picking up fleas.

"I can't power walk in high heels," was dear wife's first complaint.

"Imelda Marcos would envy your collection," I pointed out, to no avail. So it was off to Spencer to buy a pair of power walkers. After she'd talked me into a pair too, the total bill came to $84.60. Poor Brutus would have to wear what he had.

On our Big Four road, anything more than a school bus and maybe a pickup at the same time is considered a traffic jam. Without fear of traffic, we thus could walk briskly a half-mile to the curve and the half-mile back, giving us a grand total, for starters, of one mile of brisk walking. Right? As I pointed out to dear wife and Brutus when descending the driveway, unless we walk briskly we might as well remain on the couch with our feet on the coffee table. (Actually, Brutus remains on the couch only when we're away, and we have yet to catch him with his feet on the coffee table).

The reason we got off to a relatively slow start could be laid to my having noticed on a recent visit to Washington that most joggers carried weights in their hands. Assuming that this was to exercise their arms rather than for self-defense, we had stopped by the shed. For dear wife I chose a gallon can of anti-freeze and my tool kit, while I took on the sledge hammer and the hydraulic jack. With Brutus running ahead, we made it clear to the road and perhaps 30 feet beyond before deciding that we would postpone the exercising of our arms until our legs had been perfectly toned.

Once the weights had been deposited, we really hit our stride. All the way to the big maple tree. After we dragged Brutus away from there, he took off through the brush on the other side of the road with his nose to the ground. Five minutes later we heard that urgent bark he has of indicating he has just treed a moose.

While my other companion waited, I followed the racket down swales and over dales, through Canadian thistles, poison sumac and thickets of briars to where I came upon Brutus happily excavating a hole that had been dug by the grandson of the woodchuck that had walked off the Ark. He was glad to see me. I tried to keep in mind that he reportedly is my best friend as I power walked him back to the road and back to the house—where we later found him on the couch.

On my return, I found dear wife coming up the drive. Power walking her back to the road, we really now went into high gear. Just the two of us, man and wife, homo and sapien, chins up (that's one for me, two for her), setting out to overcome flab, cholesterol, blood pressure, and all other obstacles to health, home, longevity, the flag, Mom's apple pie, and all good stuff like that. I had somehow failed to remember, however, that ours wasn't the only dog along the road.

One of the Miller's dogs had been named Little Henry because his deceased father had been crossed, or double crossed, by a Shetland pony. Little Henry, however, was little no longer. In fact, when he put his paws on my shoulders, I noticed that we were about the same height. While I was trying to unload the beast, Baxter, the Abrell's dog, came up to greet us.

Baxter is a basset hound, one of those dogs said to be born under a bureau—they can't grow up, so they grow long. Little Henry got down off my shoulders to prove his dominance over Baxter. Dukes, Miller's three-legged dog, seized the opportunity to get in a few licks for himself (leaving us to speculate that Baxter might have been making fun of his handicap).

To me, this was a normal everyday doggie free-for-all. When it was over they would all go off together to tree a moose. But dear, compassionate wife, of course, had to wade into the melee to straighten things out. By the time she had got Little Henry tied up and patched up the relationship with Duke and Baxter, I was asking myself if that $84.60 might not have been better applied on a treadmill.

But at last we were off again, man and wife, etc., lowering our cholesterol, loosening the steam valve on our blood pressure, and "larding up the land," to quote a humor writer by the name of Shakespeare. We might even have powered our way past Abrell's house without stopping had not dear wife noticed that both the sun and a half-moon were in the sky at the same time.

"How come?" she said, stopping to gaze skyward. "The moon is lighted by the sun, right?" That's right, I said. "Then why isn't all the moon lighted? You took astronomy so tell me that." So I told her. (I would tell you but you probably wouldn't understand it; I wasn't sure of it myself.) Anyway, by the time we got started again I had ground my teeth down to where I might never be able to eat corn on the cob again.

At least we now had clear powering all the way to the bend in the road, our turn-around spot. Oh, yeah? Not when Abrell's "cute" white-faced steers are in the corral. And, oh look! One is coming up to the fence to be petted. When the cute beast stopped short of the fence ("the poor thing is a little shy"), dear wife, of course, had to open the gate and make the final approach.

How far we and Baxter and Duke chased those four cute capering critters before finally getting them penned in Strouse's barnyard, I can only guess. And I'm conservatively guessing about four miles. Doug Dyer trucked them back to Abrell's corral for a mere 25 bucks.

On our way home, my dear wife's bad knee went out.

"I'll get the wheelbarrow," I politely offered.

"Don't be silly," she said.

"How about the garden cart?"

She didn't answer.

With her arm around my neck, we began our debilitated walk homeward, appearing to all the community that I was bringing my wife home from an all-night bash.

Power walking a mile should be completed in, I believe, something like 10 minutes. We made it in just over an hour and a half.

The good news is I lost three pounds. What my blood pressure might register, is another matter. In my current frame of mind, it's best not to know.

Chapter 26

HOBBY HORSES

"Now that I have retired," Lois injected into my reverie on the sofa, "instead of letting our ten acres go to weeds and our barn to mice, I think we should let them go to miniature ponies and give me a hobby."

In response to my blank stare, she said: "Look at all the hobbies you have—hoeing the garden, sawing down trees, chopping wood, mowing lawns, pulling stumps, digging up the drain...

"You know I hate horses," I interrupted, for perhaps the second time in our marriage. (I have learned that if I let her keep talking, she will eventually wind down and forget her original theme.) "Remember the farmer I told you about who had fed his horse for 20 years? While he put oats in the manger one morning the horse showed its appreciation by biting off his ear, lobe and all. And did I ever tell you about Minnie, a girl I went with before you got lucky and nailed me?"

"Not over 40 times," she replied.

"To refresh your memory," I said, "I reached under her tresses to dally with her ear, only to find I had chosen the side that didn't have one. Her pet horse, in a playful mood, had beaten me to it."

"And the poor girl had to carry her earring in her hand. I've heard that 40 times too. But you won't have to worry about losing an ear to these ponies," Lois assured me. "They only come up to your waist."

The next day, I came home to find dinner still unthawed and Lois taking a crash course in raising miniature ponies, courtesy of five books checked out of the Spencer library. The day after that—or maybe it was the same day (you know how time flies when the blade of the guillotine is on the way down)—three living, breathing ponies were wrestled out of a van and manhandled through a gate leading to our back ten acres. (From my vantage point atop the woodpile I could see that the man handling them was wearing a stocking cap pulled well over his ears.) The two females couldn't be your prudish, strait-laced ponies with impeccable morals, of course. Oh, no. These two were right off the streets, both ready to "drop" their colts, as Lois phrased it, within the month.

The male's problem, as it turned out, was not a temporary bladder condition, as the dealer had explained. The little feller walked with his hind legs crossed because of a permanent case of stringhalt. This meant we would be supporting an oat burner incapable of performing his procreative duties. For mixed emotions the situation had to rate right up there with watching your mother-in-law drive over the cliff in your new Rolls-Royce.

To her credit, Lois flung herself into her hobby with a fervor she hadn't shown since she was named block chairperson for Girl Scout cookies. And she maintained that fervor for—oh, it must have been upward of three weeks. I could check it by calling the *Spencer Evening World* and asking for the date when the temperature dropped to 20 below zero. It coincided with the date of her decision to come out of retirement and to resume her nursing duties. Also coinciding with this was that our hilltop haven had suddenly been converted into a 13-acre snow cone.

"How can you work all day and take care of the ponies too?" I asked in my husbandly innocence.

"They only need to be fed hay and grain morning and night, and the barn has to be cleaned out," she replied. "And don't forget to take along a teakettle of hot water to thaw out their drinking tub."

She failed to mention that should the kettle of hot water by some miracle survive the slips, slides and plunges through the snow piled between house and barn, it would be used to thaw the barn door so it would open. This means the one who hasn't returned to nursing duty is required to slip, slide and plunge back up the hill for a second kettle of hot water to thaw the water in the tub.

The thrill of getting the barn door open on your average winter day was all any man could ask, but it doesn't hold a candle to opening the barn door to a scene better left undescribed.

Slipping, etc., back up the hill, I let my fingers race through the Yellow Pages to the first vet they came to. "One of our ponies is having a baby!" I yelled into the phone.

After waiting just short of an eternity with no response, I thought perhaps the wild banging of my heart in my throat had garbled the message. So I yelled again.

"And you want to bring her to the Veterans Hospital?" a cool voice inquired. Back to the Yellow Pages.

"Is the mare having trouble?" asked the veterinarian I reached.

Do goldfish have headaches? How was I supposed to know if the mare was having trouble? It wasn't *my* hobby. "It didn't exactly look like a picnic," I told him.

So the vet drove out, told me everything was fine and that mares usually handle these matters without interference. The advice cost $35.

Maynard Good Stoddard

Four days later I shot another $35 for his reassurance that the other mare had handled the matter satisfactorily.

I pointed out to Lois that the food bill for the barn would exceed the food bill for the house, but she assured me that colts nurse for six months. It's true—they do. Mother's milk, however, soon became only an apertif that left us with five mouths to feed, not counting our own. And what we kept pouring into these five bottomless hobbies consisted of molasses-treated, 18-karat gold nuggets priced at $4.65 per 50-pound sack, oats at $4.35 per bushel and cracked corn at $3.55 per. Their tossed salad of alfalfa and clover came to $2.00 per bale.

"And what do we get in return for this outlay?" I inquired of the initiator of this pastime. "No milk, no eggs, no cheese, no butter, no yogurt..."

"If I were doing it," she who was no longer doing it said, "instead of griping about having to mow three acres of lawn every other day, I'd let the ponies do the mowing and save the hay."

She, of course, was safely away waking patients to give them a sleeping pill when I turned the ponies out on the lawn. I didn't know—because I had not read the five books from the library—that ponies won't touch plain old grass if they can lay their gourmet lips on such delicacies as beet greens, lettuce, cabbage and Brussels sprouts. By the time I had coaxed, prodded and bribed all five into the confines of the barnyard, everything edible in the garden had been eaten. Everything not edible had been trampled beyond redemption.

The hobbyist's next bit of brilliance was buying halters (custom-made for the colts, of course) and rope so I could stake the ponies in the areas I wanted mowed. Houdini himself couldn't have escaped from those halters any faster. Pint, the stringhalted male, rose above his handicap long enough to pull his stake from the ground and wrap his trailing rope around my dwarf Red Delicious tree, converting it into a dwarf clothesline post.

"If you would do more bribing with apples and less persuading with that elm-tree limb, you might have better luck," Lois said with her usual outpouring of sympathy. "Ponies love applies." I hunted up a bushel basket and gave her a dollar to buy apples. She came home that night with six apples and 11-cents change.

The one good thing about feeding apples to ponies is that you no longer have to bother trimming your nails. Once your nails have been reduced to the quick and you have no more apples, ponies will chase you around the barnyard and try to sample your arms and legs. On the day Lois came home to find me backed into the barbed-wire fence, she opened her sympathy valve again to explain that nipping is the only way ponies show affection. "They can't very well wrap their arms around you," she said as she unsnagged my pants and patted, in turn, all five of my adoring fans on the muzzle.

Speaking of fences, neighbors on either side of us have verified that ours are not pony proof. Gail Abrell, however, verified it at 2 a.m. "Your ponies are in the road," he said, after I had hit my shin on the coffee table and hobbled to the phone, a superstition that's supposed to ward off bad news.

I woke Lois, stuck a flashlight in her hand and in the moonlight led her down the road until we spotted two ponies ready for their version of Trivial Pursuit. An hour later, as we approached our driveway, I snaked around in front to head them off. They liked this game even better. While I stood in the middle of the road, waved my arms and shouted threats, they shot past in the ditches on either side, kicked up their little heels and snorted in derision at my futile efforts.

They then managed to find the hole in Clinton Abrell's fence and went into the woods. Lois said, "Let 'em go—I've got to get up in a couple of hours." But who could go back to sleep now? It was around 4:30 before they finally grew tired of playing and returned home. Here they were warmly greeted by our ponies, who had come out of the barn to see what all the commotion was. As it turned out, the ponies I had been chasing half the night belonged to Clinton Abrell.

"It's not only that I have wandered half of Indiana by moonlight chasing the wrong ponies," I said at breakfast that morning. "But what, besides barked shins, nipped arms and free fingernail trimmings, do we get for nurturing your hobby?"

"Fertilizer for the garden, for one thing," she replied as she handed me the toast to scrape.

I said, "The whole thing is fertilizer, as far as I'm concerned."

"And what do *your* hobbies set us back?" she parried as she routed the next batch of toast directly into the wastebasket. "Your crosscut saw was nearly $30, and how much did you pay for that roto-spader—$300? Then figure the snow blower, your wheelbarrow with the pneumatic tire, your aluminum extension ladders, your long-handled pruning shears, the Weed Eater, the riding mower..."

That's one thing about a man's hobbies. He can always find some way to relieve his frustrations—like going outside to dig up an elm-tree stump. At least that's what *I* did.

Chapter 27

NOT ALL THE TURKEYS

ARE IN THE OVEN

Did you happen to read the newspaper account of an injured man in Avellino, Italy, who was riding unattended in an ambulance when he fell out and had to hitchhike the rest of the way to the hospital?

Well, you are looking at a man who can relate to such an inconvenience. Although I've never fallen out of an ambulance—not yet, anyway—the way things have been going it would not surprise me if I did.

We're talking here of such things as what should have been the simple procedure of sawing a dead limb off a scraggly redbud tree out by the road. In falling, however, the limb knocked off the ends of the top two horizontal boards on the board fence. To nail the boards back in place, I could either walk around to the gate and work from outside the fence, or I could stick my head between the boards and nail them back in place without going to all the bother of walking around. I chose to stick my head through, naturally, and work from the near side.

All well and good, right up to when I was to withdraw my head—and discovered that it wouldn't withdraw.

My head at the moment being close to the right-hand post, I couldn't get sufficient leverage to knock one of the boards loose using my right arm, where the bulk of my muscle is stored. And transferring the hammer to my left hand succeeded only in raising a blister that, had it broken, would have ended the drought on our front lawn. The only solution was to slide my head between the boards over to the left-hand post, where I could employ my muscular right arm.

Again, all well and good until my neck encountered a sliver of a length that stopped just short of penetrating my aorta, which would have opened the floodgate to my blood supply. It was the first lucky break I'd had in a month.

After withdrawing my neck from the sliver and by wearing my nape raw pressing against the top board, I finally arrived at the left-hand post. Now all I had to do was pound out the two rusty spikes holding the top board to the locust post while avoiding having the board bang against my head and affect my state of consciousness.

Traffic on Big Four road leading into the blinker-light settlement of Freedom, (Indiana, that is) most days is limited to the school bus in season, the mail carrier, and maybe a couple of pickups. But now that my head had been trapped in the fence, half of the population of Sweet Owen County found reasons for driving past. A friendly people, Hoosiers, they all waved, of course, and some even shouted pleasantries as they contributed another layer of dust to my snared noggin.

It was while waving back to Wally and Alma Walters that I dropped the hammer. And after scraping most of the hide from the inside of my right arm attempting to retrieve it, I saw my dear wife tripping past on her way to the mailbox.

"What are you doing?" she gaily asked. "Looking for mushrooms?"

After vowing that if I ever remarry it will be to a woman with Velcro lips, I replied, "No, I'm playing stocks."

Returning with the mail, she said, "Stocks?"

"Yes, stocks—where Pilgrims had their heads locked in for working on Sunday and spitting on the sidewalk and other atrocities."

"Oh," she said, shuffling the mail, "Do you want your bills here or shall I take them to the house?"

At this juncture, to my recollection, our own pleasantries ended. I remember her explaining that considering the way I do things, how was she to know that I'd got my stupid head trapped in the fence. And I recall asking her how she'd like a free face-lift. At which point she picked up the hammer and began assaulting the top board, apparently failing to notice that the pounding caused my head to bounce around like a dribbled basketball. My neck is still restricted to a ten-degree swivel.

Thus we were not on the best of terms when it came to planting the garden. If she hadn't mistaken kitty litter for Miracle-Gro, heaven only knows what would have happened.

I had already excavated holes in our billiard-ball clay to accommodate 12 Better Boy tomato plants, which alone would have furnished tomatos for half of Franklin Township. So why did she stick in another row of cherry tomatos right next door? Because they are cuter than those big old things. And when my back was turned, she snuggled eight hills of pumpkins up against my Jubilee watermelons.

So what did we get? I'll tell you what we got. We got cherry-tomato vines that practically wiped out my chivalrous Better Boys. Which meant that instead of state fair blue-ribbon two pounders, we dined on tomatos of a size that takes at least 28 to make a dozen, if you know what I mean.

As for the pumpkins, why, unless she owns a hog farm, would any woman in her right mind—but we won't go into that—plant *eight* hills of the lousy bullies? For the excitement of competition in a vine-traveling contest? If so, she gets the checkered flag. It was her villainous vines that kept my rows of carrots, beets, cabbage, and cauliflower in the shade all summer. Another hill of ruffians nearly strangled my poor cucumbers, melons, and Butternut squash. You never saw such deformities: curled cucumbers that could have passed for green horseshoes, melons that looked more like cucumbers, and dwarf squash too small even for doorstops. I tried one.

If that wasn't traumatic enough, I spent the summer tripping over pumpkin vines on my way to the shed. I pulled one of her vines out of the shed where it had tried to lay its pumpkins in the motor housing of my mower. I reeled in pumpkins that had strayed across the line fence into Abrell's pasture. In chasing raccoons out of the Hale Haven peach tree one night, I bashed my head against a pumpkin, the vine of which had sneaked up the trunk and gone out on a limb to blossom and bear.

"At least we'll have a few hundred pumpkin pies to show for all this flora," I remarked with resignation, judiciously removing my hat before my head swelled to the point where it wouldn't come off and I'd have to go to bed with it on—which would clash terribly with my pajamas.

"Pies?" exclaimed the perpetrator of the pumpkin patch. "I'm not making pies from pumpkins when I can buy pie pumpkin in a can for 75 cents."

I should have thought of that. And didn't I know that pumpkins for jack-o'-lanterns were now selling for $4 and $5 a shot? And didn't I realize that our two great-granddaughters had never had a jack-o'-lantern? No, I didn't realize that. But did we have to atone for that neglect by raising pumpkins that would endow them with at least 40 (and counting) jack-'o-lanterns each? The answer came in the form of a loud sniff.

During this time, apples were getting ripe. Have you ever picked apples while your dear wife held the ladder? I first tried to arrange the foot of the ladder on level ground. Failing this, dear wife solved the problem by shimming the low side with a piece of two-by-four, the underside of which was thoroughly rotten. The result was a real scream...from old hubby, that is, who was halfway up the ladder before the shim broke and who managed to keep his rib cage intact only by clasping one of the main limbs on his way down.

Because this cleared most of the apples on the lower part of the tree, and because no way would I remount the ladder for the apples higher up, the project appeared to be over. But never count out a woman possessing my dear wife's ingenuity. After studying the situation for no longer than a week, she decided to pick the rest of the apples using my golf-ball retriever. Her ingenuity also succeeded in removing all the metal fingers the retriever employs to grasp the golf ball. Anyone want to buy a real good three-section back scratcher for giraffes—cheap?

Perhaps this episode wouldn't have caused me to overdose on nerve tonic had it not followed so closely another tree fiasco. I refer to an attempt my dear wife and I made to keep the robins from robbin' the cherries from our big old North Star cherry tree.

We had spent the entire morning following her instructions on how to maneuver a basketball-court-size canopy of cheesecloth over the tree, she standing on one side of the tree, me on the other. Finally, after all attempts had failed, dear wife hit upon the clever idea of knotting one corner of the cheesecloth around a rock and throwing the rock over the tree.

When I came to, she told me I shouldn't have been standing so close. She also indicated that I was lucky the rock hit my head or I might have been hurt. I said how would she like a free face-lift? So we were right back where we were when I had my head caught in the fence.

Where we'll go from here, who knows? I'm guessing that the situation will improve. It had better. My space for lumps has all been taken.

Chapter 28

WAKE UP,

IT'S TIME TO GO TO BED

At the time I was plighting my troth, or troughing my plight, however that goes, a young man's choices were pretty well limited. There was the homebody skilled in the art of cooking, dusting, and raising kids, or there was the rare career girl, whose range of careers ran the gamut from schoolteacher to nurse.

In opting for the nurse, I never stopped to think—honestly—that the schoolteacher works only nine months out of the year as opposed to the nurse's opportunity of working seven days a week year round. Or that some nurses work two shifts year round. Or that until I got on my literary feet, however wobbly, this extra income might come in handy.

It *had* crossed my mind that by joining plights with a nurse, I would be locking in free nursing service for the rest of my life, or until death did us part, whichever came first. I mean, here was a woman who would coddle me at every hangnail, show compassion at every headache, run for a Band-Aid at every razor scratch. And just between us—I wouldn't want this to go any further—I had heard a rumor that for passion, no mammal on earth could hold a candle to the *Homo sapiens* female nurse.

To all of which I now say, "Hogwash!" with a capital "hog."

Taking last things first, the passion theory went down the drain when she came sagging through the door after her first post-marriage eight-hour shift. Turned out that after eight hours of tending to the demands of sick sapiens, she was up to here with sapiens, both feeble and in fine fettle.

And then there was the Hippocratic oath, which commits every nurse to the dumping of the bucket of disinfectant—also known as hospital cologne—over her head before leaving for home. One whiff of that stuff is enough to bank the fire of a man's passion for at least the next 24 hours.

The free nursing service I'd been counting on was shot down the morning a can of Alpo rolled off the kitchen counter and landed across three of the best toes on my naked right foot, already blue from the cold linoleum. I figured that before news of the pain could reach my brain computer terminal, she would have assisted me to the nearest chair, drawn a bucket of warm water, rustled up the Epsom salt, and had her arms around me in case the pain would cause me to begin hopping around and possibly break a leg.

If she had any such fears she managed to mask them behind a facade of ear-splitting laughter. Between shrieks she cried, "You should have seen the fellow we had in traction yesterday...Both legs in casts clear to his hips...Did you hurt your toes?"

No fooling—I could come into the house with my head hanging by a thread, and she would still leave it up to me to find the Elmer's glue. And while I was applying the glue she would tell me about a guy coming into Emergency that day carrying his head in a Wal-Mart shopping bag.

In the confusion of choosing the appropriate wife, I had failed to consider that a nurse might be bringing her work home with her. Especially at mealtime. Especially when we were having stew. Whereas a schoolteacher would be discussing the proper positioning of a predicate adjective, a nurse says, "I saw my first evisceration today."

With my first slurp of stew poised in midair, I say, "That's nice—what's an evisceration?"

"They took this guy's insides out. Would you please pass the steak sauce?"

I managed to eat a few crackers, but they didn't go down easy.

Even having overlooked these major surprises, I still had to consider the no-small matter of what I choose to call plain old creature comfort. What you choose to call it is your business.

You know how nurses in the movies and on the tube are always showing up in the patient's room to coax him to have a slug of orange juice, fluff his pillows, rub his back, pull up the covers, and coo, "Now you try to get some sleep," and then tippytoe out of the room? All that solicitude, believe me, ends at the patient's door.

One of the greatest pleasures in the life of a married nurse is catching hubby napping on the sofa at the end of the nine o'clock movie, jerking the pillow out from under his head, and cackling, "Wake up—it's time to go to bed!" If my nurse ever tippytoed when I was sleeping, I'd know I was still dreaming.

Then, however, thanks to a bleeding ulcer, it became my turn to take up residence in the Bloomington (Indiana) hospital. Have you got a minute?

Through exercise and diet, I had managed to reduce my baby fat by ten pounds and was about to receive my reward by stopping at the Spencer Dairy Queen for a Hawaiian Blizzard. Naturally, I was feeling good—God was in heaven, the hillside dew pearled, that sort of thing. But no more had we stepped through the door than I said to my dear wife-nurse, "You'll have to order; I've got to sit down." Which I did, laying my head on the table.

The next thing I knew, the table was covered with blood, blood was running off on my new white shoes, my wife was trying in vain to sop up the torrent with paper napkins, a boy was hurrying with a mop, and patrons right and left were suddenly losing their appetites. My nurse later said I had no pulse; the ambulance people could get no blood pressure.

Had I been in the mood for conversation, I would have asked how anyone could register blood pressure when the last of his blood was ruining his new white shoes and the stream was already inching toward the door.

But instead of experiencing the great adventure of death, I wound up in the emergency room with a nurse coaxing me to swallow a plastic garden hose intended to siphon off the last few drops of my vital juice. Another nurse was busily engaged in stripping me down to my shorts.

When my dear wife showed up, I managed to mumble, "This girl took off my pants. Do you want to say anything to her?" To which dear wife replied, "I've taken the pants off a lot of men." This brought all activity in the room to a screeching halt until my red-faced mate explained that she also is a nurse.

I won't bore you with the details—if I haven't already—of how the doctor exposed my innards with a flashlight, how he discovered what he said was a *big* ulcer, leaving me to speculate that it must be about the size of a regulation Frisbee. Turned out to be the size of a quarter. Big enough, anyway, that I spent the next four days languishing in the hospital, surviving mostly on gelatin, and trying to forget that gelatin comes from horses' hoofs. And trying not to think where horses' hoofs have been.

What I'm getting at—and it has certainly taken long enough, I'm sure you are saying—it was during this stay that I would learn why a nurse-wife has eccentricities unlike those of, say, a schoolteacher-wife.

In taking the oath upon graduation, a nurse evidently swears that neither rain nor sleet nor dark of night will keep her from waking a patient at least four times during her eight-hour shift. No matter that sleep might do the patient more good than the pill she is serving in that little plastic cup—the pill must go through. The blood-pressure people cleverly time their intrusions to fall midway between the pill servers. One nurse woke me one night—no kidding—just to ask how I was feeling.

In an effort to outsmart the night owl Nightingales, I tried sleeping during the day. Tried is the definitive word. The parade of doctors, nurses, nurses' aides, candy stripers, flower arrangers, gelatin stewards, custodians, IV replacers, and TV adjusters through my room made a beehive by comparison look about as active as a muskrat house in the Sahara.

How I was allowed to sleep long enough to dream on my last night there is a mystery. But I'm sure heads will roll because of it. Have you got another minute?

In this dream a prospective patient would save money by not routinely accepting admittance to the first hospital where the ambulance people delivered him. If his wits were still intact, he would ask for their price on whatever he had that needed fixing, then have the ambulance driver take him to other hospitals in the area for comparison shopping. So in this dream, I was occupying a bed in the hospital of the lowest bidder.

To keep the prices low, the hospital was on a cost-cutting kick. To save heating costs as well as nurses' time, two patients with the same problem were in the same bed. I was in bed with a fellow ulcer sufferer so both of us could eat from the same gelatin bowl. In the next bed were two men with their legs in traction, one right leg, one left, both hoisted on the same trapeze.

Convalescents got their therapy by helping out around the hospital and cut their hospital bill at the same time. Female patients were cleaning bathrooms, making beds, stirring gelatin, carrying trays, doing the laundry. Their male counterparts flexed their muscles polishing floors, emptying trash, washing windows. I dreamed I had been assigned the windows on the sixth floor, outside, and I was standing on a scaffold and trying to see through my hospital gown, which the wind was whipping over my head.

On one of the windows I saw posted the hospital's business hours: "Open Monday through Friday 8 a.m. to 7 p.m.; Saturday 9 a.m. to 12 noon; closed Sunday. In case of emergency, especially ulcers, try not to bleed until you can get in line on Monday morning."

When the nurse awakened me for my 2 a.m. pill, I might have kissed her except that she had already stuck a thermometer in my mouth.

On my dear wife's daily visit, I reversed tradition and gave her a bouquet, one I had spotted in a deserted room on my therapy walk that morning. Dear wife, of course, was overcome with this display of affection, especially when I explained it was my way of apologizing for her nursing nonchalance at home. She was even more overcome when she happened to find a card tucked away in the foliage, a little card that read: "Get well soon, Boss. I miss you." It was signed, "Your best friend, Spot."

I'm not sure that a schoolteacher-wife's reaction would have been any kinder or gentler. She very carefully placed the flowers on my chest, then ever-so-gently folded my hands over the stems. It was only a little thing, but the gesture will no doubt influence the rest of my natural as well as unnatural life. Especially on those nights when I am awakened on the sofa and dragged off to bed.

Maynard Good Stoddard

Chapter 29

ON SATIN SHEETS

For smarts, giving my wife free rein to choose her own anniversary gifts rates right up there with letting a shoeshine boy run off with a $5 bill to get change. But I got to thinking of the good judgment she had used in selecting me for her lifetime running mate. (We are of the old school, needless to add, when a woman took a man for better or for worse, not for everything he had.) And I decided she would come up with nothing more impractical than maybe having her ears pierced. And that only because we had recently noticed the graffiti on a downtown wall: "Ears pierced while you wait, 50-cents—3 for $1.00."

However, a couple of weeks before the big event, we were sitting there on the sofa one night when she put down her purling and dropping and said, "You know something I would really like, Barnyard (the pet name she always employs to mellow me up)? Ever since I was a little girl, I've wanted to sleep on satin sheets."

Well, well, well, well. No houseboat on White River, no trip to Hawaii, no Russian sable coat clear to the floor or no mutilated ear lobes. Just a simple pair of satin sheets; maybe 20 bucks at the most. How do you spell relief? I spelled it R-E-L-I-E-F.

After she retired that night, I looked up an ad I remembered seeing in a *Playboy* that I had taken away from our grandson to burn. (I hadn't realized that awful thing would be so hard to light.)

"Share with the one you love the luxury of satin sheets," went the pitch. "Experience the intimate, inviting elegance of satin... After 20 years, we know what we are doing in bed... Seven sensuous colors...$20 the set."

The next morning, I shot off an order for a set of sheets in sensuous blue and pillow slips in sensuous maize. (True, these happened to be the colors of Michigan, my school, but none were offered in sensuous green or white for Michigan State, where she had flunked her course in Pickle Canning II.)

In all fairness, I must confess that nothing can convert a man's humble dwelling into Buckingham Palace or his humble wife into Princess Diana like a set of satin sheets. How the lovelight in her eyes reflected their shimmering luxury. What promises they held, far too celestial for the earthy occupations of sleep, etc. (Actually, I needn't have been overly concerned about either—and not at all about etc., because etc. never had a chance.)

The first hint of having jeopardized our pursuit of happiness for this look of elegance occurred when I sat down on the edge of the bed to remove my slippers, and the pillow came sliding down to meet me. No pillow that I had known had ever been that friendly. None had even met me halfway. I slid it back where it belonged and reached for my other slipper. And here it came again. Cozied right up against me. I shoved it back again and blocked it with a slipper until I could lie down and anchor the thing with my head.

Reading in a satin-sheeted bed with your head propped on a doubled-up satin-encased pillow is not unlike laying your head in the cradle of a slingshot and having it ejected in slow motion. Before so much as turning the first page, I had oozed down completely beneath the covers. After scooching back into the light for the third time to no avail, I said to heck with it and stayed down, bringing my knees up to my chin and holding the covers up with my feet in order to get enough light to read by. Lois, who had taken an extra 15 minutes in the bathroom preparing for the realization of her childhood dream, found me in this somewhat unorthodox position when finally she came to bed.

"Why did you wait until now to do your exercises?" she inquired.

"Just couldn't wait to hit these sensuous sheets," I said, pulling her pillow out from under the middle of her back and holding it in place until she settled. As this had meant moving my head to the extreme east end of my own pillow, it suddenly squirted out and shot over the nightstand. The rustling behind me, which indicated that the woman with the childhood dream was having no better luck, was of small consolation.

Once we had turned off the light and settled our brains for a long winter's night, it required no more than five minutes for the pillows to work their way out from under our heads (that's one head apiece) and sail off into the darkness. After one scouting trip in which I ran into Lois feeling around for her pillow and liked to scared us both to death, I suggested sticking two-way tape on our cheeks and foreheads. The proposal was defeated by a vote of 1 to 1. So I turned my pillow lengthwise, like a sack of wheat, and placed my head gently—ever so gently—on the top end. I might as well have been hugging a greased otter.

Eventually, thanks to a state of sheer exhaustion, we both managed to doze off. As later reconstructed, my pillow immediately seized the opportunity to spring out and slap Lois full in the face. Her first impression was that I was trying to smother her. This in turn sent the top sheet and cover flying to parts unknown. We knew where, of course, when we turned on the light: They were draped over the vanity.

At 2:58, by the clock, everything was back in order. By 3:10, the cover of our remade bed had skidded off the top sheet and taken up residence on the floor. And Lois, in turning over, had cocooned herself in the sheet, leaving me protected from the elements by nothing more than pajama bottoms and the few scraggly hairs on my chest. Not that it really mattered.

Percale people will never appreciate how lucky they are to climb into bed with some assurance they will stay there all night. But without velvet pajamas, or clinging to the headboard, or bracing against the nightstand, I defy anyone to remain in one place on a satin sheet for 15 minutes. And when the bed is swayback, as ours is swayback (I could mention whose back has swayed it, but she would deny it), make that ten minutes. Should there be any free time after chasing your pillow, retrieving the cover or competing for the top sheet, it is spent clinging to the edge of the mattress or climbing out of the trough in the middle if you relax your grip.

The morning after our initiation, while we were making up the bed, I offered a few suggestions to whom it might concern. One was to pack her dream away in the attic with the other relics of her youth. The alternative: cut some strips from our outlawed studded snow tires and glue them to the sheets and the underside of the pillows. She said don't be silly, and did that other pillow go under the bed again?

It did. But that was only one of the reasons I was late for work that morning. Standing on opposite sides of the bed, we smoothed out the bottom sheet and drew up the top sheet. Then Lois captured the pillows and held them in place while I pulled up the cover. This left Lois with the option of releasing the pillows or being covered with them. She chose to release the pillows. By now, the top sheet was hanging on the bias on her side. While trying to get it righted, she saw the pillows begin sliding and let go of the sheet to grab them. Her language was by this time becoming improper, so I let go of the cover to help her. The cover seized the opportunity to slide off the end of the bed.

The next laundry saw the satin sheets go into the closet and the percale returned to the old swayback.

Satin sheets do have one advantage. It was Ben Franklin who said, "Fish and house guests smell after three days." With satin sheets on the bed, guests aren't likely to test the three-day mark.

Fortuitously, it was a visiting couple from Lois's side of the family that made the mistake of mentioning that they had never slept on satin sheets. No kidding. Nothing to do but give them a taste of good old Hoosier hospitality by digging out the satin sheets and turning our bed over to them, while we roughed it on the convertible sofa.

I had never slept well in the thing anyway (much practice as I had), so it mattered little that the commotion and conversation emanating from the adjoining room penetrated the wall with ease.

"Have you got both pillows?"
"No, I think I heard yours hit the nightstand again."

"Could you possibly spare a little of the cover?"

"Me! I thought *you* had it."

It was beautiful...until about 4 a.m., when we heard that sickening thud, which we interpreted as something more than a pillow hitting the floor. Having abandoned all hope of sleep, the foolish couple's thoughts had lightly turned to romance.

When we rushed in and turned on the light, there they lay, blinking in bewilderment. The pillows, fortunately, having preceded them, neither was hurt. Physically, at any rate. We spent the rest of the night playing 10-cent skit-scat. They left right after breakfast.

All things considered, maybe I've made worse investments than that 20 bucks for satin sheets. We have a lot of relatives on Lois's side of the family.

Chapter 30

A SPRIG OF MISTLETOE

Trying to explain through a closed bedroom door is bad enough. Trying to explain through a closed bedroom door that has been locked, bolted and barred is even worse. But lying out here on the sofa at least gives me a quiet interlude to improve on my defense.

Reconstructing the evening, it had gone like this:

"Where's the mistletoe?" I called from the living room, where I had assumed command at the last minute.

"What mistletoe?" Lois answered from the bedroom, where she was in the final throes of dressing.

"The mistletoe you were to get to hang over the door. You *know* how sentimental Jim and Helen are about stuff like that!"

"Oh dear!" she cried. "I'm afraid I forgot it!"

"Then I'll have to run over and get some?" I screamed.

"Take the car!" she shrieked. "They'll be here any minute—you know the Haines." The Haines have the bothersome habit of always being on time.

Take the car! For a lousy sprig of mistletoe? With a supermarket carrying such stuff only a block away? I could run there and back while sorting out the ignition key on my key ring.

Had I needed a shopping cart, there wouldn't have been one on this side of Cape Hatteras. But now that I was after nothing but a lousy sprig of mistletoe, there were abandoned carts all the way to the store. I fell over the first one no more than 10 feet from the back gate of our apartment. The parking lot was full of carts. There was even one with four good wheels inside the store. But all I wanted was one lousy sprig of mistletoe.

The trouble began in the bread department. How I ever managed to spot them, considering the pace I was setting, I'll never know. But there were those dark rye buns Lois had been looking for. Two packages. I knew if *she* had been there, she'd have taken both. So I did.

Then destiny led me to the "Tiny Tom" turkey.

Now, some people don't know it—including most turkey breeders—but your average turkey is just too much turkey for a family of two. Especially when one of the two would just as soon eat a kelp casserole. Oh, I don't mind honoring our national bird on *its* day. And I can tolerate a dark-meat sandwich that evening. But after turkey hash, turkey soup, and a grand finale of turkey omelet, I put my fork down.

Here, however, was a turkey raised in a shoe box—or maybe stunted from smoking while still a poult. It weighed in, according to the label, at a mere 5 pounds, 7 ounces, stripped. Even then I might not have grabbed it up had it not been the only runt in the bin and had this woman in the rigors of shopping fever not been going for it at the same time—cocksure, shopping list, cart with four round wheels, kid in the basket—you know the type. And when she addressed me with a look that would have kept the entire meat section at the correct temperature for a week, I'd have claimed the bird had it been a 50-pound, 7-ounce buzzard.

How many of you have ever carried a frozen turkey without benefit of cart? Could I see the hands? That's what I thought, no hands. Lost them to frostbite, didn't you? I made it only as far as the bacon display before dropping that 5-pound, 7-ounce ice cube and my two packages of dark rye buns and sticking my hands under my armpits. But lucky me, I had set the stuff down on a one-hour special: bacon at only 99-cents a pound! How proud of me Lois would be if I came home with a pound at that price. And prouder still with two pounds. I took three.

By the time I reached the virtual *giveaway* on tomatos (which were themselves giving way, I learned too late), the turkey was supported by the two packages of dark rye buns, now flatter than a ruptured football bladder, and the once flat bacon had returned to its original shape before leaving the pig.

Had the tomatos been advertised at something less than five pounds, maybe the bedroom door would not have been locked tonight. But I'm the type of shopper who doesn't argue with a sign. If it says so many for so much, I take the so many—in this case five pounds of over-the-hill tomatos.

Then, in corralling my other selections, I found that I had rested them on a crate of Texas watermelons. Watermelon for Christmas! Lois would *love* it!

Whatever else you may think, give me credit for a little common sense. No way would I have taken on a watermelon had it not been for this abandoned cart at the end of the meat counter. Assuming that someone, upon seeing the day's price on sirloin steak, had passed out and that the counterman had thoughtfully carried the passee into the cooler until help arrived, I assumed command of the cart.

However, no sooner had I got everything nicely loaded, except for the tomatos, than this woman of average belligerency appeared from behind a leaning tower of cat food and exclaimed, "What do you think you're doing with my cart!"

At that moment, I thought I was dropping in a five-pound sack of tomatos. And thanks to her, I was dropping it from a height that sent a full two pounds squishing out through the bottom grid. The woman departed in the direction of a booth labeled "Manager."

In trying to get the mess cleaned up before the manager's arrival, I was observed—by a husky young chap changing the price on jars of instant coffee—using a mop from a display conveniently nearby. So instead of returning the mop to the rack, I thought it prudent to add the thing to my purchases.

And that's how I came to clear the shelf of Wesson oil.

As I suggested to the manager, if supermarkets would post STOP signs, or at least YIELD, at intersections, things like this just wouldn't happen. As it was, this woman—you remember the woman who lost out in the Tiny Tom turkey competition?—came charging out of nowhere and caught my cart broadside, and the handle of my mop practically wiped out a shelf of Wesson oil. Only one bottle, luckily, failed to make a safe landing on the 7-Up cartons below. But one was plenty.

In fact, should Ralph Nader have the Wesson people on his hit list for giving short measure, he can forget it. The Wesson people have somehow managed to put two gallons of oil into their 16-ounce bottles, which is more than enough to coat a dwarf turkey and a watermelon, inundate two packages of dark rye buns and three pounds of bacon and have the stuff running out of a sack of tomatos at the check-out counter.

I suppose a valid argument could be made that what followed was basically my fault, as I did most of the bagging—the bag boy being tied up chasing my watermelon around the counter. But finally I left the store with everything snugly nestled in two double-strength sacks, each nicely balanced, the mop under my arm and confident that I was as good as home. Thirty feet later, the turkey sack let go.

It could have been worse. And shortly it was. Enough of the sack had remained intact to contain the other items, and I was able to support the turkey against my chest. Ever support a frozen turkey against your chest? Really frosts your organs, doesn't it? Especially when it keeps sliding down around your knees. In working it back up for the third time, the other sack ruptured and began spewing tomatos at a rate of one every ten feet. The watermelon, having landed on my foot, suffered nothing more than a cracked end.

Consequently, my arrival at the outer door of our six-unit apartment complex was not what could be called impressive. The turkey, fairly well thawed by now, lay cradled in my unconscious left arm. My right arm embraced the melon and the mop. The one remaining sack, clamped between the turkey and the melon, was still leaking tomatos one by two.

Working the door handle with my conscious elbow, I finally managed to get a foot wedged in and swing the door wide enough to squeeze through. All but the mop. The handle didn't make it. Snapped off about halfway up, I hoped Lois would be so enraptured with my other purchases she wouldn't notice.

In retrospect, the situation would have been improved had she not flung open our apartment door just as I was gathering myself to knock with my forehead the second time. Otherwise I wouldn't have ended up in the hall closet in that jumble of coats, turkey, sweaters, dark rye waffles, umbrellas, tomato puree, boots, bacon blobs, rubbers and a short-handled mop. The watermelon, fortunately, had scooted out of sight behind the sofa.

"They're here!" hissed Lois, in that manner of hissing that wives reserve for husbands at such moments. "Where's the mistletoe?"

When the issue of whether or not I would be sleeping in the bedroom tonight was weighed, I believe now that I have gone over everything, what counted most heavily against me was looking up into those beady brown eyes and responding, "What mistletoe?"

THE END

About the Author

Now that my first two masterpieces, *Everything is So Close We Can Even Walk to the Carwash* and *Putting My Best Foot Backwards*, have mesmerized the reading public, the few still out of thrall have begun clamoring "MORE! MORE! OH, GIVE US MORE!"

Therefore, I have given up my daily grind of bikini spotter on Panama City Beach (Florida, of course) for the purpose of selecting another 30 gems from the 158 I have rendered for *The Saturday Evening Post*. The title: *Nothing Serious, I Hope*.

If you like what you read, I ask only that you tell your friends, your neighbors, and your relatives—even those you don't particularly care for. If you don't agree with my outlook on marital predicaments, I would appreciate it if you kept it to yourself. Perhaps I can repay you sometime. During bikini season, that is.

Printed in the United States
3713